IMAGES
of America

JOLIET'S GERLACH BARKLOW
CALENDAR COMPANY

On the cover: This is an early photograph of the Gerlach Barklow Company employees preparing to ship the next year's new calendars. The lady in the front is propping up one of the new calendars. Thousands of local Joliet-area men and women were employed by the calendar company over the several decades that it operated in Joliet. (Authors' collection.)

IMAGES
of America

JOLIET'S GERLACH BARKLOW
CALENDAR COMPANY

Tim and Michelle Smith

ARCADIA
PUBLISHING

Published by Arcadia Publishing
Charleston SC, Chicago IL, Portsmouth NH, San Francisco CA

Library of Congress Control Number: 2009931249

For all general information contact Arcadia Publishing at:
Telephone 843-853-2070
Fax 843-853-0044
E-mail sales@arcadiapublishing.com
For customer service and orders:
Toll-Free 1-888-313-2665

Visit us on the Internet at www.arcadiapublishing.com

This book is dedicated to our family, which has always supported our passion for collecting and researching the Gerlach Barklow Company. We would also like to dedicate this book to two people who possessed the same passion that we have for collecting calendar prints from the Gerlach Barklow Company. Both these enthusiastic collectors have now passed away; however, we will never forget the fun we had with these fellow Gerlach Barklow collectors and good friends. We will miss them both immensely. See pages 125 and 126 for the dedication to these two wonderful friends.

CONTENTS

ACKNOWLEDGMENTS

We have enjoyed being passionate collectors of Gerlach Barklow prints, paintings, and memorabilia for several years. Starting with just a few calendar prints purchased from the local antique stores and shows, our passion has grown to include collecting the actual calendar paintings that were used to produce the prints. The real enjoyment of collecting this artwork comes from the people we have met and the friendships that have flourished along the way, as we continue on our journey to collect illustration art. As we write this book, our hope is to document not only the history of how the factory grew to become one of the largest calendar companies in the world but also to tell the story of some of the wonderful employees that were employed by the calendar factory. We want to thank Dick Murphy for his additional insight on the operation and workings of the calendar company. We also want to thank our friend Linda Carlson for her assistance with the "Lois Delander, Joliet's Miss America 1927" chapter in the book. Almost all the photographs and prints in this book came from our private collection.

INTRODUCTION

Former successful calendar salesmen and employees Theodore R. Gerlach, K. H. Gerlach, and Edward J. Barklow set out to own their own calendar business. This led to the organization of the Gerlach Barklow Company. While they may have entered the calendar-manufacturing field in a limited manner in terms of their personal finance, they realized the importance of sufficient capital to manufacture quality calendars and products. The original idea was to form the company with a capital of $100,000, but it was decided it would be better to start with $200,000. When the decision to form a company was made, Theodore R. Gerlach and Edward J. Barklow had so little money that they used a kitchen table from Barklow's home as their business desk. They were fortunate to secure the cooperation of people who could furnish not only the money but also the mature business judgment. At the head was Col. John Lambert, a self-made man who had fought his way from laborer to president of American Steel and Wire Company of Joliet. This later became part of United States Steel Corporation. In 1887, prior to becoming a calendar salesman in Iowa, Theodore had owned an independent tea and grocery store in Joliet near the steel mills, operated by Lambert. It is thought that they had known each other through being businessmen in Joliet in the late 1880s and early 1890s. Dr. J. C. Flowers, a successful Joliet businessman and friend of Lambert, joined and supported the financing of the Gerlach Barklow Company. A few years later, in 1909, Flowers was instrumental in establishing the Economy Motor Buggy Company in Joliet, manufacturing the very early Joliet automobiles.

The Gerlach Barklow Company was incorporated in June 1907, and the factory was built the same year at Washington and Richards Street in Joliet. The first few months were strenuous ones. The work of building a modern plant, installing machinery, purchasing materials, selecting paintings, making engravings, preparing samples, and above all assembling a sales force were all Herculean tasks. This was all accomplished in a six-month time frame, after the company was incorporated and producing calendars for the 1908 year. In the present day, the building permits and approvals to construct a plant of this size could not be completed in six months, let alone the completion of a building with the production of calendars. If there ever was a doubt of success, the second year of calendar sales in 1909 doubled, and the Gerlach Barklow Company was on its way to becoming one of the largest calendar companies in America. In the next two years, the factory building received two additions, each as large as the original building, making the 100,000 feet of floor space the largest factory in the world devoted to making art calendars. In 1917, the company was capitalized at $2.5 million, and by 1928, the factory floor space had grown to 330,000 square feet. The 1923 Gerlach Barklow review booklet has pictured in it a Canadian factory in Stratford, Ontario. This factory was purchased in 1920 and remodeled to suit the requirements of the business.

In 1924, the P. F. Volland Company of Chicago merged with the Gerlach Barklow Company and began printing books and greeting cards in Joliet. The P. F. Volland Company was best known for its children's books, notably the Raggedy Ann series. It was also one of the few companies to use the arts and crafts style of graphics on many of its greeting cards. During the 1927–1928 time frame, the Gerlach Barklow Company of Joliet entered an agreement with Rolph-Clarke-Stone of Toronto to begin producing calendars so it could handle more of Gerlach Barklow's market outside the United States, printing both in English and French for customers in the province of Quebec.

The company survived the Great Depression of the late 1920s and 1930s and actually grew in size and sales during this time period. In the 1940s, sales skyrocketed, and the company did very well with the emergence of the glamour girl and pinup calendars of the 1940s and World War II. During the 1950s, the greeting card division became part of the Rust Craft Greeting Card Company of Dedham, Massachusetts. In 1959, the Shaw Barton Company purchased the Gerlach Barklow Company. The Shaw Barton Company had been one of Gerlach Barklow's competitors during the 1940s and 1950s. Shaw Barton closed the plant sometime after purchasing it. The plant sat idle and fell into disrepair over the next several years. Unfortunately, in 1992, the building caught fire and was destroyed. A housing development was later built on the property.

Over the lifetime of the company, Gerlach Barklow manufactured primarily calendars, ink blotters, and children's books. It also specialized in advertising items such as desk/pen sets and leather goods. Its art calendars included the work of some of the world's foremost artists of the day, both American and foreign. The artworks of famous illustrators such as Zula Kenyon, Adelaide Hiebel, Bradshaw Crandell, Philip Goodwin, Atkinson Fox, Rolf Armstrong, and Jules Erbit have graced the calendars of Gerlach Barklow over the years. Throughout the company's existence, Gerlach Barklow emphasized quality artwork and prints. Today the original paintings and prints produced by the Gerlach Barklow Company are sought after by collectors across America.

One

THE FORMATION AND SUCCESS OF THE GERLACH BARKLOW COMPANY

In June 1907, the preliminary steps were taken to organize the Gerlach Barklow Company. The prime movers in the organization were Theodore R. Gerlach, Edward J. Barklow, and K. H. Gerlach. For years, all three men had connections with one of the older calendar companies in Iowa. Theodore and K. H. knew the sales side of the calendar business from their previous employment as salesmen. Barklow had the experience of dozens of years of managerial experience, along with thoroughly being familiar with every phase of calendar manufacturing. Next these gentlemen secured the cooperation and financial backing from two Joliet businessmen, Col. John Lambert and Dr. J. C. Flowers. At this point, they had the financial support to start the company. Lambert was named the first president of the Gerlach Barklow Company and remained in that position until 1919 when Theodore R. Gerlach became president. Flowers was named the treasurer of the company and remained at that position until the 1930s.

Construction began on the calendar factory in July 1907. The building was ready for occupancy in November of that same year. Two wings were added to the building within a few years. Despite a slowdown during World War I that delayed the building of a new warehouse until 1919, the company continued to grow. The calendar sales did well over the next 20 years as advertising was expanding in leaps and bounds, due to printing improvements of the early to mid-20th century. Every household in America had a calendar advertising a local business attached to the wall or icebox. Previous to the invention of the television, there was no better way to advertise a business than to have one's business name hanging in kitchens where families sat and ate their dinner each night. This is a tradition that remains today in many homes across America. The company was founded on the principle that "We Ourselves the Better Served by Serving Others Best." This principle moved the company steadily forward over the next 50 years.

GENERAL OFFICES AND PLANT, JOLIET, ILLINOIS, U. S. A.

The Gerlach Barklow Company incorporated in 1907, and the factory was built the same year. Theodore R. Gerlach and Edward J. Barklow had traveled to the East Coast to purchase paintings to be used as calendars in the late summer of 1907. This was accomplished in order to get the sample calendars out in front of the customers prior to the upcoming year of 1908. This drawing pictures the new factory during an era where horse and buggy as well as the automobile occupy the street. It was a time of imagination, initiative, and boundless energy. (Authors' collection.)

The Gerlach Barklow Company building grew to a building with nine acres of floor space. The lettering on the water tower pictured above the building in this photograph reads, "The Gerlach Barklow Co. Art Calendars for Advertising, Joliet Ill." The company advertised that "the main doorway to the building lead to the general offices and factory of the company, where quality art calendars are produced for a nation of advertisers." (Authors' collection.)

T.R. GERLACH
VICE PRESIDENT

E.J. BARKLOW
GEN. MANAGER

JOHN LAMBERT
PRESIDENT

J.C. FLOWERS
TREASURER

HENRY B. BALE

OFFICERS and
DIRECTORS of
THE
GERLACH-BARKLOW
COMPANY

H.L. THOMPSON

K.H. GERLACH
SECRETARY

The first officers and directors of the company are pictured in this early company review booklet. Col. John Lambert, the president of American Steel and Wire Company, was at the head of the financial group and first president of the Gerlach Barklow Company. Theodore R. Gerlach is listed as the vice president, K. H. Gerlach as secretary, and Edward J. Barklow as the general manager, along with Dr. J. C. Flowers as treasurer. In addition, Flowers was also a Joliet physician and was instrumental in starting the first automobile factory in Joliet, known as the Economy Motor Buggy Company. Since the majority of the money to start the company was provided by Lambert (president) and Flowers (treasurer), they controlled the finances during the early years. Director Henry B. Bale is listed in the Joliet city directory as a lawyer living on Union Street. H. L. Thompson is listed in the 1909 city directory as treasurer of the Woman's Mutual Benefit Company, along with Flowers being listed as president of the same company. Little is known about K. H. Gerlach other than that he was a salesman at the Osborne Calendar Company prior to becoming an officer with the Gerlach Barklow Company. It is known that K. H.'s first name was King. He lived on Third Avenue in Joliet in 1909. He later moved to Western Avenue. (Authors' collection.)

Theodore R. Gerlach is working at his desk in this photograph. Born in 1867 in Mount Vernon, Indiana, he began his business career as a clerk in a tea store in Detroit and was subsequently employed as a clerk in a grocery store in Chicago. In 1887, he established himself as a grocer merchant in Joliet. He was a calendar company salesman from 1892 to 1907 and is listed in the 1896 Joliet city directory as a traveling agent (salesman). He is listed as living at 501 Richards Street. Years later, he built the calendar company on this same street. He organized the Gerlach Barklow Company in 1907. He was vice president of the company until he purchased the interests of Col. John Lambert and became president of the company. Gerlach married Charlotte D. Hill in 1889. Her father was a congressman and assistant attorney general of Illinois. The couple did not have any children. Charlotte died on September 18, 1925. Theodore did remarry a short time before his death in 1933. He was a Republican his entire life and also enjoyed fishing and hunting. (Authors' collection.)

Edward J. Barklow was born on January 16, 1867, in a log home built by his grandfather near Freeport. When he was a child, Barklow's grandmother thought he should have a more complete name than Eddie and asked him to select the name he preferred; he chose Edward. Since his father's name was Joseph, he added that as his middle name. As he grew up, he generally used just his initials and became known as E. J. or Ed. Barklow attended the Northern Illinois Normal and Dixon Business Schools. He worked for the Osborne Calendar Company of Red Oak, Iowa, and was the assistant manager when he left to join Theodore R. Gerlach to start the Gerlach Barklow Company. Barklow wrote a hardcover book that was published in 1928. The book was titled *The Log of the Beloved Adventures*. The book details his travels through Asia and Oceania. (Authors' collection.)

Theodore R. Gerlach was very involved in various companies and was very active in the local community. Gerlach was the director of the Ferndon Manufacturing Company, an advertising sign company of Aurora. He was vice president of the Joliet Wrought Washer Company, along with being president of the Commercial Trust and Savings Bank of Joliet. He served as president of the Joliet Chamber of Commerce, president of the Advertising Specialty Association, trustee of Silver Cross Hospital, and president of the Joliet Country Club. The first official telephone call through the Joliet telephone dial exchange was made around midnight on August 20, 1932, with Gerlach; A. H. White, Joliet district commercial manager for Illinois Bell; state senator R. J. Barr; and John T. Clyne, vice president of the First National Bank of Joliet, in the room. Previous to this call, all Joliet telephone calls came through the Chicago exchange. (Authors' collection.)

The Theodore R. Gerlach home pictured above was built in 1913. Western Avenue was home to Joliet's elite businessmen and their families during this time period. This area is still currently considered one of Joliet's more historic areas. Gerlach lived in this house until his death in 1933. A unique part of this home was the bank vault that contained a full liquor bar inside of it. The house was purchased in 1939 by mobster Francis "the Slim Man" Curry. Curry reportedly was a very close friend of Tony "Big Tuna" Accardo, who was a well-known godfather for the Chicago syndicate for many years. The Col. John Lambert home pictured below was on Herkimer Street in Joliet. It was considered to be a mansion when it was built. The home had stained-glass windows and a wine cellar, and the entire third floor was a large bedroom. Lambert founded and built the Joliet Public Library. A large pastel of Lambert, done by Gerlach Barklow artist Zula Kenyon, hangs in the library. (Authors' collection.)

Richards Street, where the calendar company was built, was named for David Richards, a local landholder, farmer, and dairyman. Richards was born in Herkimer County, New York, and was in the dairy business before coming to Joliet. He came to Joliet by horse and wagon. He helped start the Joliet Woolen Mill. The Richards frame home was located where the Gerlach Barklow factory stood. The frame home was moved twice, as additions were made to the factory building. This house had been built by Richards around 1860. David Richards donated the property for the Richards Street Methodist Church. David's brother Charles came to Joliet sometime after David. Charles was a very successful local doctor and served as the Will County coroner. (Authors' collection.)

Two

CALENDAR MANUFACTURING AND THE EMPLOYEES

The Gerlach Barklow Company employees included the artists, salesmen, and retouching artists. However, a majority of the people worked in the following departments: watercolor tinting, photography, pressroom, offset transfer, cutting, raw stock room, inspection, power plant, finishing, and shipping. The factory employed as many as 1,000 men and women, along with having over 500 sales personnel across America. One of the main reasons Theodore R. Gerlach chose Richards Street in Joliet for building the calendar company was due to the large number of women that lived in close proximity. In 1907, when the calendar factory was built, the majority of women did not drive an automobile and often walked to work.

The Gerlach Barklow Company was very active in the community and sponsored almost every type of sports team that comes to mind. The company held an annual employee summer picnic at Electric Park in Plainfield, as well as a Christmas party each year in a hotel in Joliet. Some 30 years after the plant closed, almost every employee commented during interviews that "the comradery at the company among both the employees and management was the best part of working at Gerlach Barklow." Many of these employees hired on just after finishing high school across the tracks at Joliet Township High School. Edward J. Barklow was credited by many of the employees for this feeling of being part of a big family, as employees of this large factory. At a time when many factories were like sweatshops, the Gerlach Barklow Company was recognized as a great place to be employed.

The company and employees did very well over the 50-plus years it operated in Joliet. The factory offered some of the better pay and benefits in the area. A sense of loyalty from both management and the employees seemed to exist during the span of the company's operation in Joliet. Many Joliet residents still feel that the day in 1992 when the abandoned plant caught fire was one of the saddest in Joliet's rich history.

The 1925 Gerlach Barklow review book states, "The artists who paint these pictures devote their lives to the creation of beauty and human interest. By their artistry, they have recreated fond and tender memories as well as bringing sunshine into the hearts and lives of millions who hang their calendar images in homes across America." Very few photographs exist of the wonderful artists who produced these beautiful calendar images. Most of these artists gained very little fame during their lifetimes and did not become recognized until well after they passed away. (Authors' collection.)

After the painting was completed and approved by the calendar line committee of five men and women with years of experience in advertising art, it was taken to the photographic studio where four great arc lights with a total of 240 candlepower were directly shown upon it. It was photographed six times through color separation lenses, which brought out every detail of the painting in correct coloring and shading. (Authors' collection.)

The glass negatives were developed and carried to a studio where most outdoor light was subdued. Here, along one side of the studio, touch-up artists worked at glass easels through which was reflected a north light. Each of the six negatives was placed in turn on one of the glass easels. It was then carefully retouched and perfected by artists whose skill and technical knowledge made them masters of their craft. (Authors' collection.)

The six glass negatives were taken to the photograph composing room where each was turned in place in a vacuum machine and with the aid of a powerful light, the impression on the glass negative was transferred to a metal plate. This technique made a positive image on these zinc metal plates. The images on the glass negatives and zinc positives are smaller than the original paintings. (Authors' collection.)

The zinc metal plate, or positives, were taken to a mechanically operated proof press. The proof operator started with the yellow and went through the entire range of colors. Specimens were printed from the original zinc plates. He proofed each one and marked corrections where necessary. They were then returned to the etcher to be perfected. (Authors' collection.)

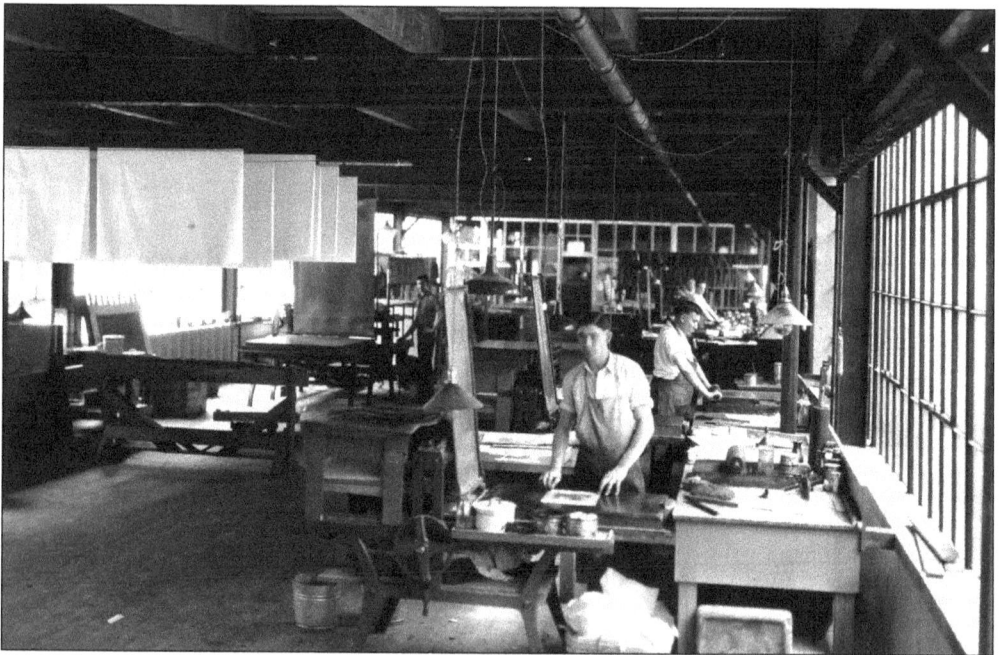

The metal plates were transferred to press plates. This large metal plate was as large as 38 inches by 52 inches, with as much as up to 21 different images. These plates only contained one color per plate, making it necessary to have six separate plates for one run of prints. A yellow, a light blue, a gray, a red, a pink, and a dark blue plate were all required. (Authors' collection.)

The press plates were carried down to a large offset pressroom where the Gerlach Barklow Company housed long rows of huge presses. Upon arriving at the pressroom, the plate was secured and clamped around the press cylinder on the large press. The opposing cylinder had a large heavy rubber blanket clamped to it. The two presses were bought together until the metal plate made a true impression upon the rubber-covered roll or cylinder. (Authors' collection.)

The sheets had to pass through the rolls once for each of the used colors, or six times. The press could hold 25,000 sheets, which passed through six times for each print or 150,000 impressions for each print run. This resulted in the sheets coming out of the press in full color. For short runs, small lithographic offset presses were used. They produced ink blotters and postcards. (Authors' collection.)

According to the 1925 calendar company yearbook, the printing presses at the Gerlach Barklow Company could run 5,000–6,000 pieces an hour, while special equipment would tie the calendar pad on the calendar automatically. Plant personnel specially trained for manufacturing their products operated the equipment. In this photograph, Edward J. Barklow, vice president of the company, watches the pressmen operate the machines. (Authors' collection.)

The finished large sheets, consisting of several images on each, were cut to size and formed in stacks of 250 sheets. This produced "mount prints" for use as calendars. Some of the cutting machines had razor-sharp 75-inch knives. The line committee determined the overall sizes, mounting styles, size of the calendar pad, and every calendar detail down to the color of the ribbon or cord. (Authors' collection.)

The composing room set and printed the advertisements onto the calendars, while the tinting department attached the top and bottom metal strips for hanging the calendars. The folding department used a Dexter folding machine in the 1930s. It was one of the latest folders on the market. This machine was capable of producing a 32-page booklet or smaller from a flat sheet of paper. It was especially used for folding items such as sample booklets. (Authors' collection.)

The inspection department inspected all the calendar prints for defects, with defective prints being thrown out. The good prints were counted, wrapped, and put on the shelves for filling orders. The shipping department had a spiral carrier system that came down from the third floor of the building. Most early calendar orders were shipped in wooden crates. Later shipments of the calendars were made in corrugated cartons. The factory stitched its own corrugated boxes. (Authors' collection.)

Nearly 100 salesmen are shown leaving the plant for the 1910 calendar campaign, each carrying their salesman sample suitcase full of the next year's calendar line. At one point, the Gerlach Barklow Company employed over 500 salesmen. The marketing and selling of calendars is truly a seasonal product. The 1912 Gerlach Barklow line booklet states the following to the business owners: "Calendars are purchased but once a year, and for the whole year, they represent you in homes and offices of your customers and prospective customers. How important, therefore, that you make no mistake in your selection of a calendar to represent your company or business." The company employed field sales supervisors for each region. Their job was to support and assist the salesmen who traveled from town to town. Below is a salesman business card for Gerlach Barklow that belonged to William Schofield, great-uncle of author Michelle Smith (née Schofield). William Schofield lived in Joliet; however, he worked as a salesman in New Mexico and Arizona. The card has the logo picturing Louis Joliet. (Authors' collection.)

The GERLACH-BARKLOW Co.

ART CALENDARS

FOR ADVERTISING

OFFICERS:
JOHN LAMBERT, PREST.
THEO. R. GERLACH, V. PREST.
K. H. GERLACH, SECY.
J. C. FLOWERS, TREAS.
E. J. BARKLOW, GEN. MGR.

EXCLUSIVE COPYRIGHTED SUBJECTS

JOLIET, ILLINOIS

W. B. SCHOFIELD

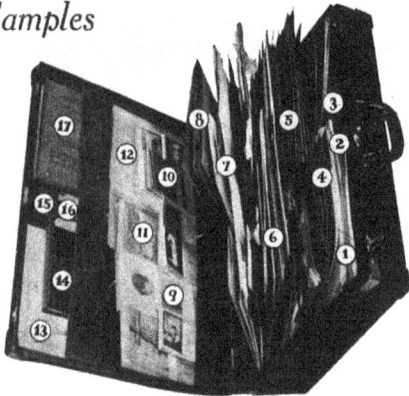

Packing and Care of Samples

KEY

1. Jumbos	7. Envelopes containing	12. Fans
2. Business Calendars	loose prints	13. Booklets
3. Art Mounts	8. Loose prints monthly	14. Price Book
4. Gold-Gravures	service series	15. Sales Manual
5. De Luxe Calendars	9. Small blotters	16. Art gum, tube of
6. Water Colors	10. Large blotters	glue, thumb tacks
	11. Monthly calendars	17. Stock copy book.

YOU can't know too much about your samples and you can't treat them too carefully! Pack them carefully and know where you pack them.

The appearance of your samples is, in a great measure, going to help or hinder sales. Carry an art gum eraser and a tube of glue, because prints will slip out and front sheets come loose no matter how carefully they are handled, and keep your samples looking neat and clean.

Another thing—don't check them on trains! Don't gamble that you won't lose by checking them! One day lost because of not having your samples with you may mean hundreds of dollars to you in lost business in the early part of the season especially.

The salesman suitcases contained samples of the various calendar lines that included the title leaves books, which were small booklets containing calendar prints from each year's calendar line, along with a brief article about the artist. Gerlach Barklow even had instructions for the salesman on how to pack his sample case. "Printed instructions include communicating the most important thing is to have a system. All business calendars should be kept together with the largest size in the back, graduating according to size so the small sizes will always be in front of the deluxe section. Unless the above ideas are carried out and samples are returned to the proper place, shortly it will be impossible to locate the sample wanted by the customer and loss of business will result." (Authors' collection.)

In the early days, the Gerlach Barklow Company specialized in hand-colored calendar prints. Hundreds of Joliet-area women were employed to hand tint the prints that would be used on calendars. Since the coloring of the prints was done by hand, no two prints were exactly the same. The company advertised the calendar hand-colored prints, saying, "These calendars are exceptionally soft and delicate. The demand of particular people for quality and exclusiveness of hand color has resulted in bringing out hand-colored or watercolor pictures. There are a few men in every line of business who are never satisfied with anything short of the best that can be produced. These ultra particular people find the best in Art Calendars in the Gerlach Barklow Hand Water Color Line." (Authors' collection.)

This Production
has been specially prepared
by the designing department
of
The Gerlach-Barklow Co.
Joliet, Illinois   :   Toronto, Canada

One former employee wrote in 1995, "The Gerlach Barklow Company and I are the same age. We both were born in 1907. While a sophomore in high school, I left school and went to work in the engraving department at Gerlach Barklow Company earning eleven dollars a week. That was a lot of money to a sixteen year old. Four months later, while walking past the high school on the first day of school I started to cry. I wished I had stayed in school. I told my boss Mr. Dodsworth, that I was quitting my job. He asked me why. I told him I had to go back to school. Good, he said I'll give you two weeks salary so you can buy your books. I'll always be grateful for his kindness to me on that day." (Authors' collection.)

The same employee later made a deal with the P. F. Volland Company in the same building to take home greeting cards and hand color them. She would pick up the cards on the way home from school and lug them home. She lived only one block from the factory. She would color them that night and take them back to the factory before school the next day. She used a kerosene lamp for lighting while working on the cards. In one example, she mixed her tints at night by the lamp but did not get them the correct color. The supervisor told her to wash off the tint and to mix the tint in the daylight, retint them, and she would accept them. This high school girl employed by Gerlach Barklow later went to college and became a teacher in Joliet. (Authors' collection.)

The company was one of the first to use what it termed as both village industry and cottage industry. This flexibility by the company allowed neighborhood women to take the calendars home and assemble them. The women would complete the calendar assembly work at home while watching their children. This was quite an innovative idea for the time period. Often the children at home would help their mothers by tying ribbons to the top of the calendars and stacking the calendars in boxes. Once complete, the finished goods were carried back to the factory where the woman would receive more calendars and ribbons to take home. During the early days of the company, most families did not even own a car. Having this factory in their backyards was a great opportunity for women to be employed. (Authors' collection.)

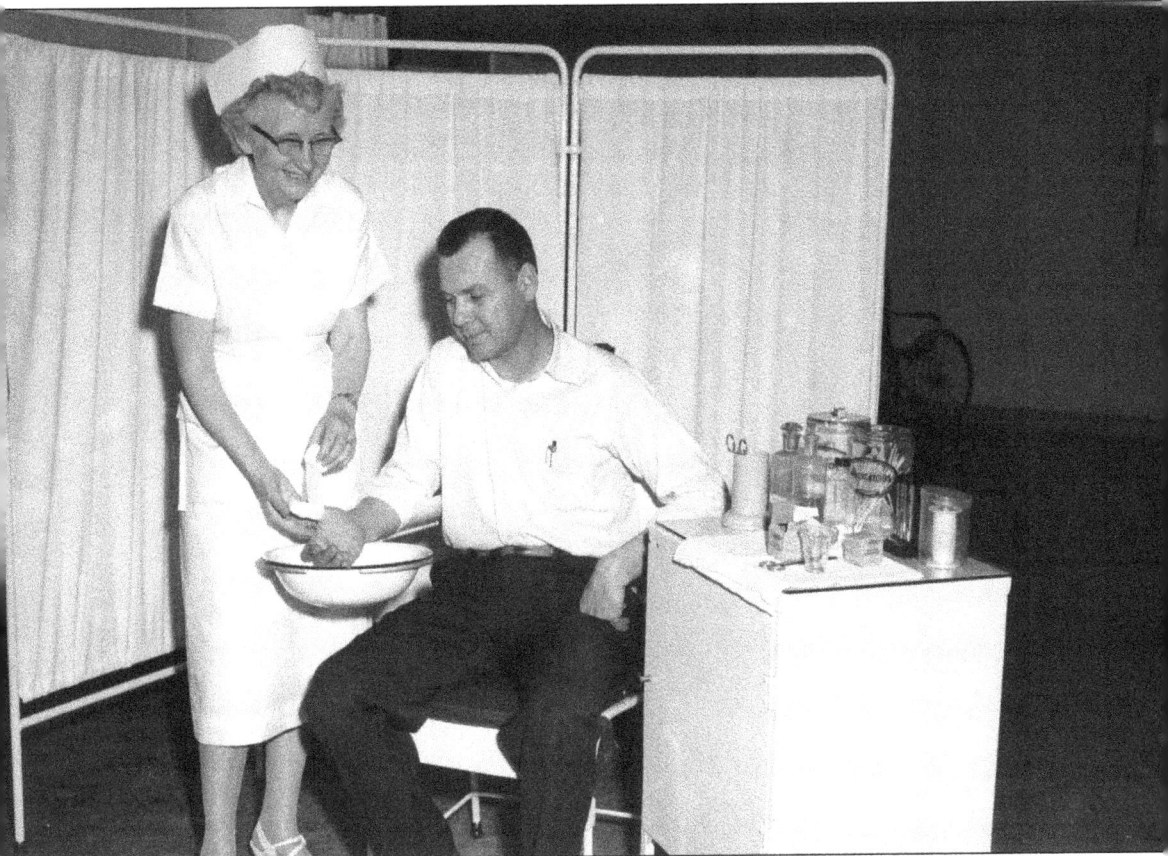

The building was designed to allow plenty of sunlight inside as well as having high ceilings, since many of the employees stayed all day at a table coloring prints or assembling calendars. The company was one of the first in the industry to employ a registered nurse who worked under the direction of a physician. In 1927, the nurse's office was referred to as the emergency hospital. The company advertised it was a modern sanitary dispensary and a necessary addition to the organization. It was on the same floor as the pressroom, hole-punching machines, and wire-stitching areas. This location for medical treatment was probably chosen due to the potential for accidents occurring in these departments. (Authors' collection.)

The art director for the calendar company worked with the artists to give them direction on which images were needed for the next year's calendar line. Harold S. Hewlett from Plainfield was the Gerlach Barklow Company art director from 1933 to 1958. Hewlett was also an artist for the company and had several published calendar prints during his career. He sometimes used neighborhood children as subjects for his artwork. In 1952, a Gerlach Barklow calendar that Hewlett designed, titled *World of His Own*, pictured his grandson James Coleman. It was painted by Adelaide Hiebel. The art director also developed names for pseudonyms for the artists. These were not the real names of the artists but names they would paint under instead of using their own names. Hewlett's son told a story of his dad using a pseudonym as the name of a man who was washing windows at the factory. Hewlett and a few of the management team were struggling to find a good name for a pseudonym, so they called the man to come inside. They asked him his name and liked it, so they used it for the name of the artist on one of their calendar prints that year. (Authors' collection.)

32

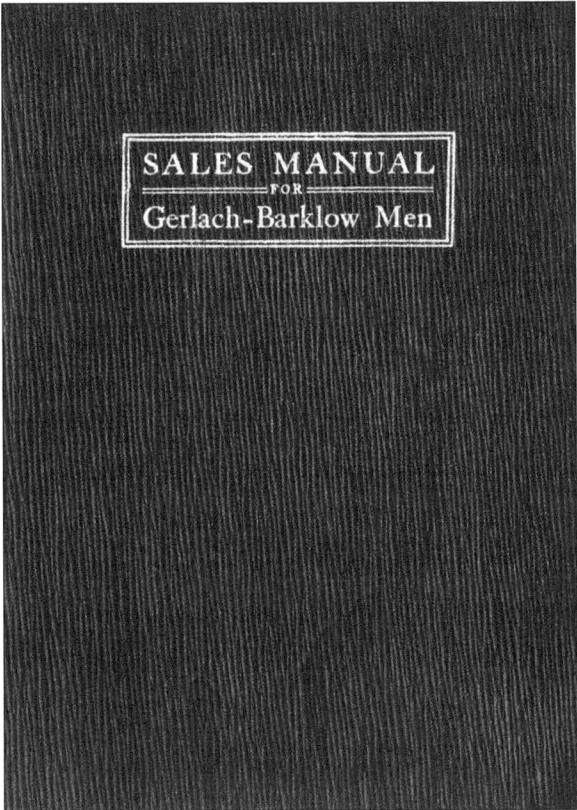

Note that the cover of this Gerlach Barklow Company 1917 sales manual has printed that it is "for Gerlach-Barklow Men." The 1920 company review book pictures and mentions saleswomen working for the company. Even during these early years, at times, the company's top calendar sales leaders were females. These books described the logic of calendar advertising, the history of the Gerlach Barklow Company, the company product lines, and places for the salesmen to go to find business. The 1921 sales manual below has the portion about being for the Gerlach Barklow men removed from the cover. Times had changed. (Authors' collection.)

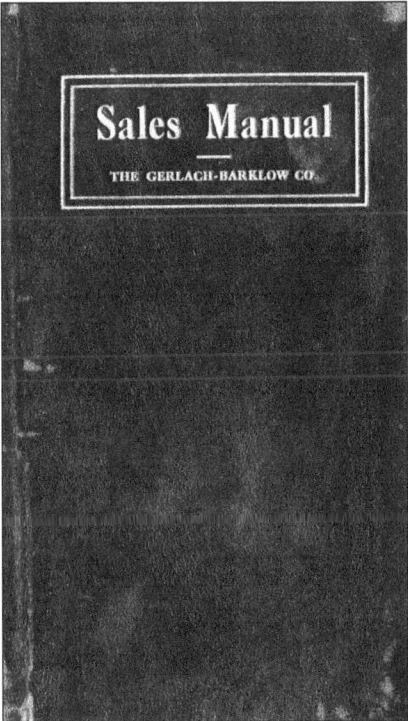

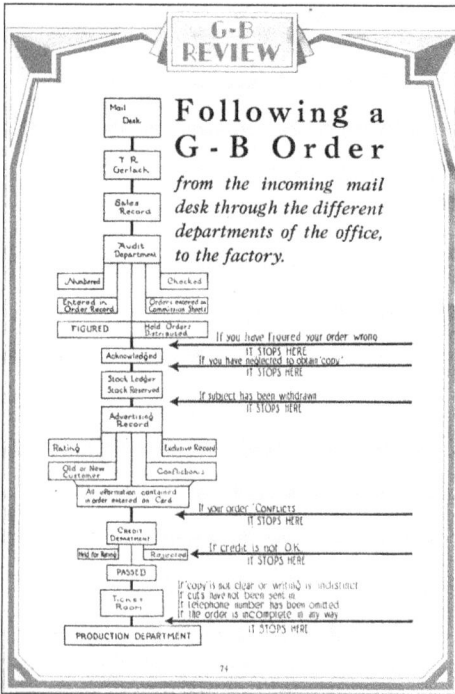

Following a G-B Order

from the incoming mail desk through the different departments of the office, to the factory.

The Gerlach Barklow ordering flow chart indicates how the order was handled prior to going to production in the early days. Note that all the orders came from the mail desk through Theodore R. Gerlach before moving forward to the order system. This is out of the 1929 Gerlach Barklow review booklet where it advertises to the salesmen, "Let us ride the wave of optimism and prosperity while making 1929 the year of years. Tremendous demand is ahead of us that will insure a very busy year in industry." This booklet was printed a few months before the stock market crash of 1929, which began the Great Depression. (Authors' collection.)

Pictured here is a 1929 Gerlach Barklow Company common stock certificate for 100 shares. This stock certificate is made out to the E. J. Barklow Company. The company would also produce a booklet for the benefit of the stockholders titled *Selling Sentiment: The Friendliest Business*. The company also gave these booklets to each employee. (Authors' collection.)

OSCAR TAPIO
Special Order Dept.

Oscar Tapio not only was employed by the company but also was a key player for the company baseball team for many years. Tapio had the foresight to save a large amount of his yearly calendar sample and review books, as well as several pieces of other company documentation. These company booklets have supported keeping alive the memory and history of this great company. Tapio also purchased several pieces of the original artwork from the company that was owned by the Tapio family for many years. Oscar's brother Enio also worked and played baseball for the company. (Authors' collection.)

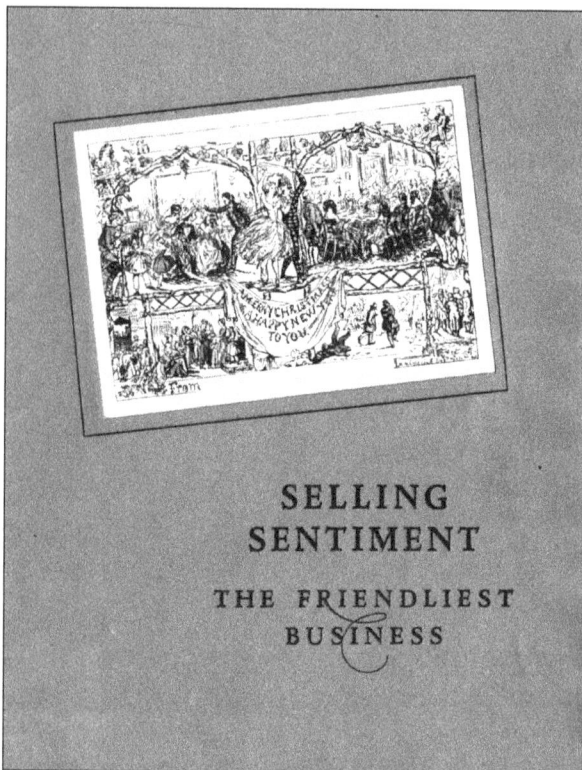

This 1946 *Selling Sentiment* booklet contains many photographs of how calendars are produced by the employees of the Gerlach Barklow Company. Inside is printed, "Please accept this booklet with our compliments. We hope you and your home-folks will enjoy the story of the development of our business during the years that have passed since it was organized in the early part of this century." (Authors' collection.)

Gerlach-Barklow Calendar Works, Joliet, Ill.
The largest of its kind in the world.

An interesting story that has been told is about a young girl who survived the Holocaust working at the company. A manager at the company paid for a young Jewish girl to travel to Joliet and work at the calendar factory. She was known as a good singer and a very talented and good-looking redhead and told the employees stories of her survival in Germany. She even wrote some articles about her experiences for a magazine. (Authors' collection.)

President,

J. C. MacKeever became vice president of the Gerlach Barklow Company in 1923. Upon the death of Theodore R. Gerlach in 1933, he was elected president. MacKeever began his career as a salesman for Shredded Wheat Biscuit Company. MacKeever had also been employed by Arbuckle Brothers and Procter and Gamble before coming to the Gerlach Barklow Company. He was very active in Joliet's civic life and had extensive experience in both the manufacturing industry as well as local association activities. In 1943, he became the president of the Illinois Manufacturer's Association. (Authors' collection.)

This photograph shows a majority of the employees at the Gerlach Barklow plant. Although not dated, it appears to be from prior to 1930. The company employed several women for every man. If was often said in Joliet that working at Gerlach Barklow was a great opportunity for a man to

find a wife. This did happen very often, with couples getting married after meeting at work. A man working in the calendar hand-tinting area could be outnumbered by women over 50 to 1. (Authors' collection.)

Pictured is the 1930 Gerlach Barklow basketball team. Pictured are, from left to right, (first row) Dick Fassino, Gordon Ellis, Cy Stark, Chick Spesia, and Joe Pereisiti; (second row) Ed Koerner, Stan Erickson, and Ed Wenck. The Gerlach Barklow Company sponsored many local sports teams each year. (Authors' collection.)

The 1935 Gerlach Barklow baseball team was the Will County baseball champion. Pictured are, from left to right, (first row) Richard Fassino, Oscar Tapio, Cy Stark, Joe Pereisiti, Fred Boseo Jr., John Pitcairn, Whitey Lawrence, and Fred Boseo Sr.; (second row) T. D. Luccock, Cash Mills, Henry Brunnings, James Talcott, ? Svetlecic, Bill James, Slim Francis, Eddie Murphy, Jack Mastalach, J. C. MacKeever, K. H. Beuret, E. J. Barklow, and John Kelly. These names are taken from a handwritten note on the back of the photograph. The team played in the local Joliet league, which included names such as the Joliet Grays (prison team) and the Joliet Telephones. (Authors' collection.)

The Gerlach Barklow Company men's bowling team members pictured are, from left to right, Ray Fahr, Joe Garavaglia, John Fitzer, Enio Tapio, and Dick Fassino. The company sponsored both a men's and women's bowling team each year. Below is an embroidered logo from a Gerlach Barklow bowling shirt. The company bowling teams also competed in the local Joliet factory leagues. (Authors' collection.)

The 1940–1941 Gerlach Barklow Company women's bowling team won the Class C Chicago American Bowling Tournament. Pictured are, from left to right, R. Grey, Bertha L. Brown, Jean Robinson-Tolle, Darraine Imfeld, and Maybelle Cooling. These names were taken from a handwritten note on the back of the photograph. For many years after the factory closed, Robinson-Tolle organized the retiree meetings, which met annually. Robinson-Tolle also owned one of the original Adelaide Hiebel pastels, which was given to her upon her retirement from the company. Many of the employees owned original paintings that were offered to them to purchase before selling them to the general public. (Authors' collection.)

The 1945 Gerlach Barklow Company women's baseball team is pictured in front of the Richards Street entrance to the building. Pictured are Rosalie Kezele, Vera May Jones, Ruth Lanham, Lillian Knowles Lucaora, Jane Knowles, Maybelle Cooling, Irene Frangen, Faye Hauck, Henry H. Brunnings, Pauline Vercellotti, Elvera Serio, and Helen Pell. These name spellings are taken from a handwritten note on the back of the photograph. (Authors' collection.)

When interviewed in the 1990s, a former employee mentioned that she had hired in at the Gerlach Barklow Company as a pressman's helper. She later was taught to run the large Gorman press before being promoted to a color plate artist in the art department. She commented that her years at Gerlach Barklow were "happy years with friendly caring people. The bosses considered their employees as family and tried to fit them into the best job possible." One of her favorite memories was of the wonderful smell of all the new paper at the plant. She attributed her experience at Gerlach Barklow to later being offered a position as a wallpaper artist at the Joliet Atlas Wallpaper Mill. (Authors' collection.)

The creation, planning, and production groups look over various images for the next year's calendars. The photograph pictures Dick Murphy, Marvin Fabring, Ed Payne, and Marie Kande. The photograph is dated January 1, 1958. The Will Rogers calendar line image is included in the photograph and the discussion. The Will Rogers series was one of the more popular Gerlach Barklow Company calendar lines for many years. The company offered a calendar with an image of Will Rogers for over 15 years. Several different artists produced the Will Rogers images over this time period. The Shaw Barton Company continued this series even after purchasing the Gerlach Barklow Company. (Authors' collection.)

The **REVIEW**

Vol. 10   July 19, 1917   No. 34

THE GERLACH-BARKLOW CO.

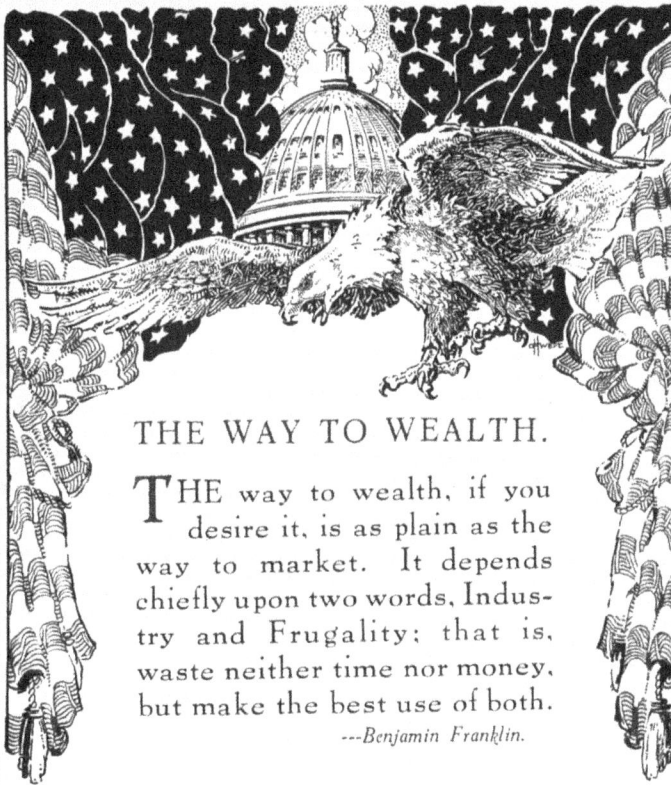

THE WAY TO WEALTH.

THE way to wealth, if you desire it, is as plain as the way to market. It depends chiefly upon two words, Industry and Frugality: that is, waste neither time nor money, but make the best use of both.

---*Benjamin Franklin.*

SERVICE · QUALITY · BEAUTY

This cover of the July 19, 1917, Gerlach Barklow review booklet had Louis Joliet on the front. The following page listed the Gerlach Barklow "Ten Commandments of Salesmanship." They were listed as "Be Agreeable, Know Your Goods, Don't Argue, Make Things Plain, Tell the Truth, Be Dependable, Remember Names and Faces, and Don't Be Egotistic, Think Success and Be Human." These sales commandments guided the sales team for over five decades. The quotation on the front of the booklet from Benjamin Franklin would also hold true today. It states, "The way to wealth, if you desire it, is as plain as the way to market. It depends chiefly upon two words, Industry and Frugality: that is, waste neither time nor money, but make the best use of both." (Authors' collection.)

THE GERLACH-BARKLOW CALENDAR

salesmaker

JOLIET   ILLINOIS

November 1954

Sunday		Tuesday	Wednesday			Saturday
29	1	2	3	4	5	6
7	8	9	10	11	12	13
14	15	16	17	18	19	20
21	22	23	24	25	26	27
28	(29)	30				

"O" DAY

golden years

**MONDAY
NOVEMBER 29th
IS 'OPENING DAY'!**

VOL. 49 . . . No. 1   NOVEMBER 25 1954

The weekly communication newsletter booklet title was later changed from the *Review* to the *Salesmaker*. It remained a weekly publication for the factory employees and traveling salesmen. This November 1954 copy mentions November 29 as opening day for the 1955 calendar sales. Inside the *Salesmaker*, it states that the factory will be "eagerly awaiting your opening day sales orders and reports." This weekly publication mentions the Orange Quota Contest, which it touts as the finest contest offered by the company where the winner is awarded a crate of Florida's finest oranges and grapefruits from the company-owned groves. The highest scorer in sales each week was also given a $10 cash credit. The top 25 salesmen for the year received a $100 watch suitably inscribed or a $100 silver serving set. (Authors' collection.)

The Gerlach-Barklow
Book
of

SLOGANS

and

EPIGRAMS

This booklet is the property of The Gerlach-Barklow Company and is loaned to you for use in connection with sales of the G-B advertising mediums.

The 1931 *Gerlach-Barklow Book of Slogans and Epigrams* contains examples from advertising slogans for the various types of business to be printed on the calendars. For a restaurant, the slogan "If you don't eat, we'll both starve"; for an eye doctor, "If you cannot see right, you better see us"; for life insurance, "Could your widow live as well as your wife does?"; for a department store, "Where your dollar has more cents"; for dairies, "A meal in a glass"; for coal, "One good ton deserves another"; for cleaners and dyers, "We live to dye, we dye to live"; for candy, " Dainty made for dainty maids"; and for a clothing store, "When you want to put on the dog, buy from us." (Authors' collection.)

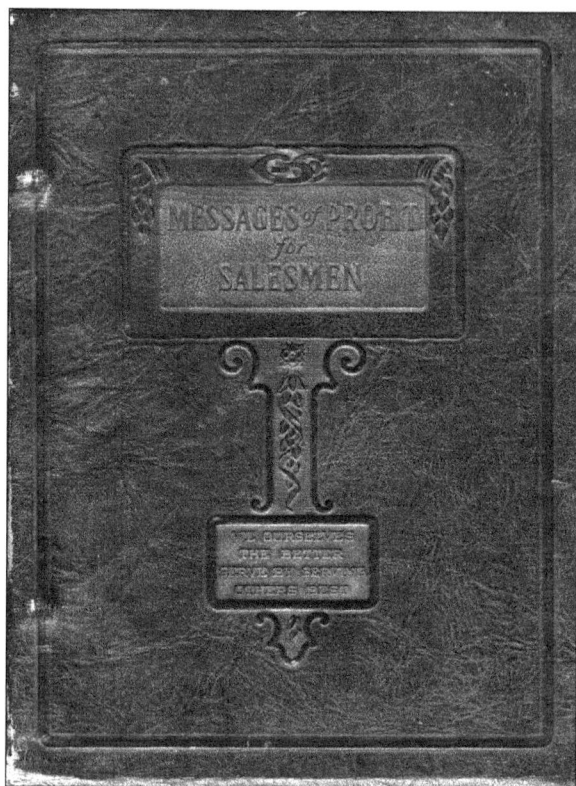

The Gerlach Barklow Company had an intense training program for its salesmen. The 1926 Gerlach Barklow Company salesman training guide is titled *Messages of Profit for Salesman*. The training manual contained topics such as "Mental Actions and Reactions," "Your Most Profitable Sale," "On Which Stage Are You Traveling on Your Road to Success?" "What Are Your Most Productive Hours?" "Imagination Rules the World," "The Will to Win," "The Biggest Word in Any Language Is Tomorrow," "Greenbacks and Confidence," "The Self Starter Generator, Optimism," "The Challenge of Price," "Guard the Profit," "Killing the Sale with Talk," "The Problem with Competition," and "Success: It's Found in the Soul of You." Below is an example of one of the training unit covers. (Authors' collection.)

Gerlach Barklow printed a Christmas booklet that detailed photographs of the company Christmas party. The inside of the booklet states, "Christmas is an important day for the Gerlach Barklow family. Our customers in thousands of communities are distributing our greeting cards and calendars during the holiday season. Millions of Americans are exchanging messages of good will through the medium of friendly cards and calendars produced during the year." Printed under one Christmas party photograph is "We will find our richest winnings in the precious love of friends." The company pushed the "family and friendship" atmosphere of the employees at every opportunity. (Authors' collection.)

Our Christmas Album . . . 1949

THE BIG TREE

This photograph of the printing department personnel was taken on July 18, 1930. The printing department at the plant was one of the few where the men outnumbered the women. The presses and printing machines were large pieces of machinery with exposed moving parts that were quick to injure the employee who was not experienced or paying attention at all times. A large plate was placed on the offset press and clamped to a huge metal cylinder. The cylinder revolved against a cylinder covered with rubber, and the impression was transferred to a rubber surface. The rubber-covered cylinder in turn revolved against a cylinder bearing the paper sheet and then

transferred from the rubber blanket to the printing paper. The sheets were lined up on the line-up table, which was used for lining and checking the proper position of the plates on the sheets of paper. The Miehle printing presses came in various sizes. Some of the presses had automatic feeders, and others press operators had to hand-feed the paper. In the 1920s, the plant installed two color presses that merely were two cylinder presses connected together; this made it possible to print two colors on the same press. The plant also installed automatic bronzing machines in 1927 that were used to put a bronze edge on the calendar sheets. (Authors' collection.)

In 1994, a former employee of the Gerlach Barklow Company mentioned in an interview that she had started working for the P. F. Volland Company's greeting card division in 1946. She remembered seeing some of the large paintings used for calendars. From time to time, she recalled that the employees would be offered an opportunity to purchase the paintings. One of her favorite places was the penthouse apartment that sat on the rooftop of the factory. She reminisced that it had a private entrance that led to a large studio with glass ceilings and walls. It had a bedroom, bathroom, and kitchen. The back room opened onto the rooftop of the building. In 1948, it was no longer in use and very dirty. She believed it must have fallen into disrepair during World War II. (Authors' collection.)

The Gerlach Barklow Company Quarter-Century Club was organized by the company in 1945 for employees with 25 years or more of service. The Quarter-Century Club held a banquet each year to honor the members. In the 1950s, the banquets were held at either the Elks Club ballroom or the Woodruff Hotel dining room. The company's banquet program listed active, inactive, and deceased members. The Rust Craft Greeting Card Company continued this club with the 1970 Quarter-Century Club program, listing 80 employees as active, 151 as inactive, and 101 as deceased members. Pictured at right is the 1955 club dinner meeting program, and below is the 1970 Quarter-Century Club program. (Authors' collection.)

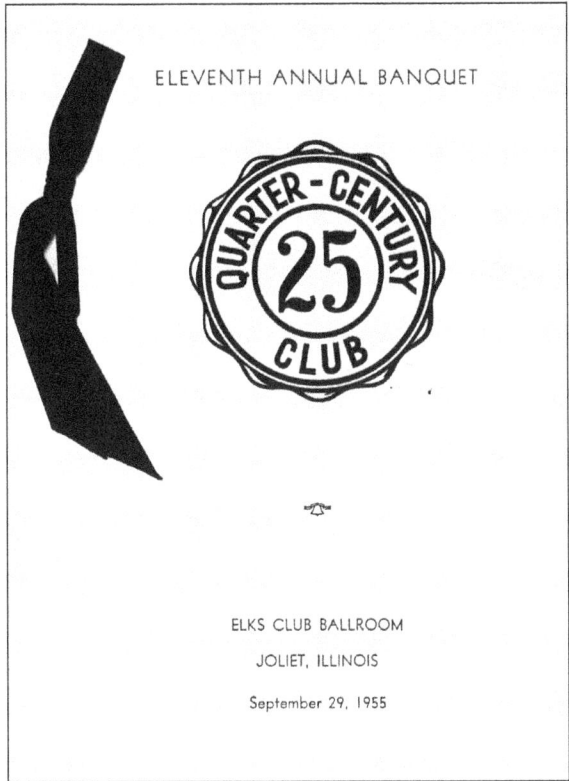

ELEVENTH ANNUAL BANQUET

ELKS CLUB BALLROOM

JOLIET, ILLINOIS

September 29, 1955

At a Quarter-Century Club meeting, one former employee spoke of how she had worked at the company for 34 years. She had started working at the calendar factory in 1939. The only job she ever had at the company was in the calendar sample department. In 1939, a friend told her the calendar factory was hiring women right away, with no waiting. She went with her friend the next day, was hired, and started working by the end of that day. Her department filled all the salesmen sample requisitions with supplies. The sample department was on the same floor as the management offices and nurse's room. She helped out in the office selling cards, calendars, napkins, and tablecloths to employees during the lunch hour. She also mentioned that the company would give each employee a two-pound box of candy for Christmas. (Authors' collection.)

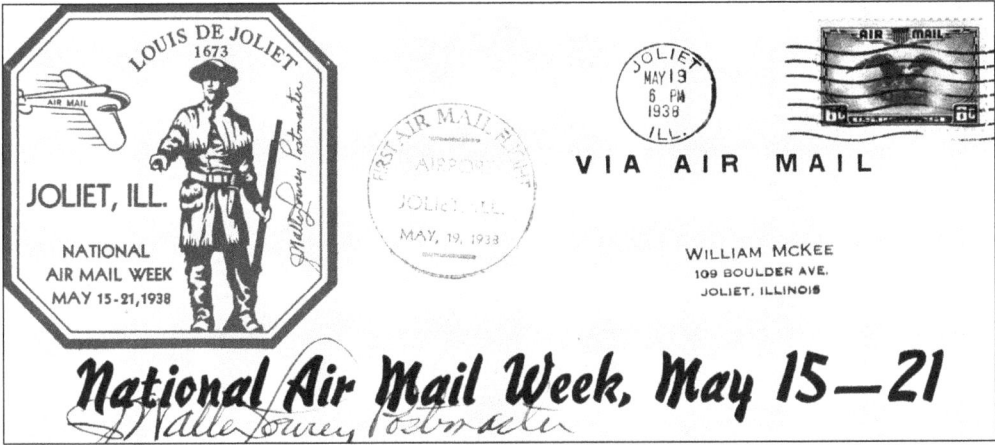

The photograph above shows the National Air Mail Week envelope from the Joliet post office for May 15–21, 1938. The picture of Louis Joliet graced the front for the National Air Mail Week celebration. The photograph below shows it was sponsored and printed by the Gerlach Barklow Company. It is also postmarked from Joliet's post office on May 19, 1938, and signed at the bottom by the current postmaster at the time. The company advertised, "There are Various Methods of Advertising. Each is king in its own particular field." Getting its name on these airmail envelopes is an example of the company working at having its name on everything possible in the local community. (Authors' collection.)

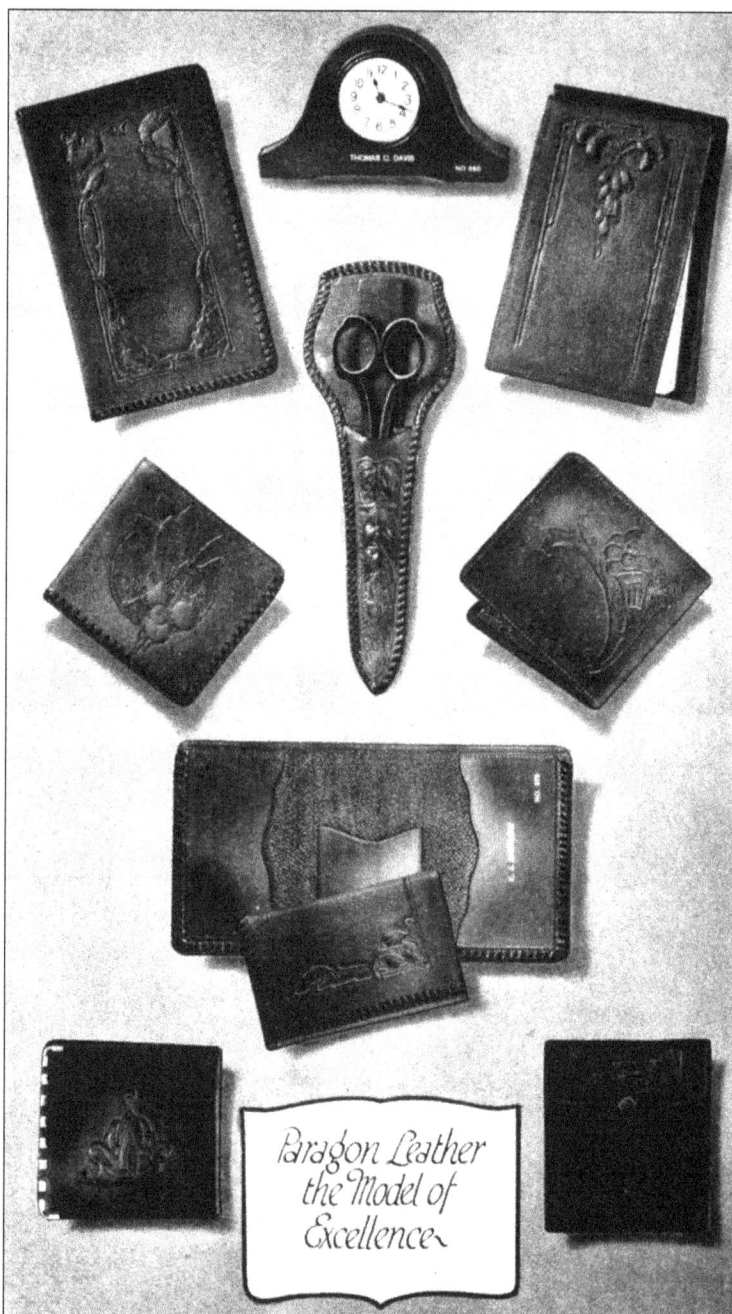

Beginning in 1924, the Gerlach Barklow Company added to its paper advertising line by producing a high-class line of leather utilities. The company completed three months of activity in 1924 in organizing and establishing a department that would create products other than calendars and blotters. Over 7,000 square feet of factory floor space was converted and remodeled to suit the needs of this new department. It purchased machinery and stock along with hiring personnel, training personnel, designing a new advertising line, and making samples for the salesmen. The idea was to place leather samples in the hands of the selling organization and begin adding profit to the company by selling more than paper products. (Authors' collection.)

The Gerlach Barklow Company's manufacturing had ceased, and the building was vacant for several years. The windows were broken out of the building by vandals during the time it sat idle. The building had been purchased by a private party. In 1992, a fire destroyed a majority of the building. The current owner did not have insurance on the property and stated that he had used all his money for the purchase of the building. The property was later purchased by the City of Joliet. The city developed the property into a housing subdivision with a $650,000 grant from the Department of Urban Development. (Authors' collection.)

The Gerlach Barklow building had to be completely razed before the construction of the new housing on the site to be named Richards Grove. Before the wrecking ball could take a swipe at the building, the Joliet police had to wake up a few men who were sleeping inside the building. They had been sleeping up near the old elevator pulley. The building, once home to a thriving art calendar company, was being torn down in 1995. The local residents simply called the brick building the Gerlach. The workers at the site later ground the concrete up into gravel that filled the hole in the ground where the factory once stood. The factory where so many people met their future spouses was demolished. The workplace so many Joliet residents depended on had disappeared by wrecking ball in a matter of just a few short weeks. (Authors' collection.)

Three

THE P. F. VOLLAND AND RUST CRAFT GREETING CARD COMPANIES

The P. F. Volland Company of Chicago was founded by Paul Fredrick Volland. The company mainly printed books and greeting cards. The P. F. Volland Company was known for its children's books, notably the Raggedy Ann series. Over the years, it employed many well-known artists to illustrate its books and greeting cards. The P. F. Volland Company used the arts and crafts style of graphics on many of its cards, as well as having many art deco images grace its greeting cards. It merged with the Gerlach Barklow Company in the 1920s and moved into the Gerlach Barklow building in Joliet. At one point, four different companies were housed in the building in Joliet under the name of United Printers and Publishers Inc. The companies under the United Printers and Publishers umbrella included the Gerlach Barklow Company, the P. F. Volland Company, the Artographic Company, and the Rust Craft Greeting Card Company. In 1959, the Shaw Barton Company purchased Gerlach Barklow. It was one of Gerlach Barklow's largest competitors.

The Rust Craft Greeting Card Company started in September 1906 when Fred Winslow Rust opened a small bookstore in Kansas City. In October of that year, he published a simple Christmas card with only a text greeting. The first letter of the first word was larger than the rest and was printed in red. This would be the style on his future greeting cards. Rust's cards were the first enveloped cards in the industry. This card sold only in Rust's bookstore and was very successful, selling 5,000 copies by Christmas. By January 1908, Rust Craft had a line of Valentine's Day and Easter cards. These cards were marketed on both U.S. coasts. By 1910, the production had grown to the point that the company closed its retail portion and focused on the creation and production of its greeting cards. In 1913, the company moved to Boston. Rust Craft was a leader in many areas of greeting card design and production, including the unusual card surfaces, colors, and sentiments. It was the first company to use braille-embossed cards for the blind. The Rust Craft Greeting Card Company operated the Joliet location for several years.

Color-separation artists Albin Zlogar of Joliet and Donald Campbell of New Lenox work on color-separation drawings for reproducing the 1958 Rust Craft greeting cards. This was one of the first steps in the manufacture of greeting cards at the Joliet plant. The Rust Craft greeting card line was made up of a diversified group of high-quality greetings, all of them different. Most designs, according to the company, were unusual in style while outstanding in beauty and quality. (Authors' collection.)

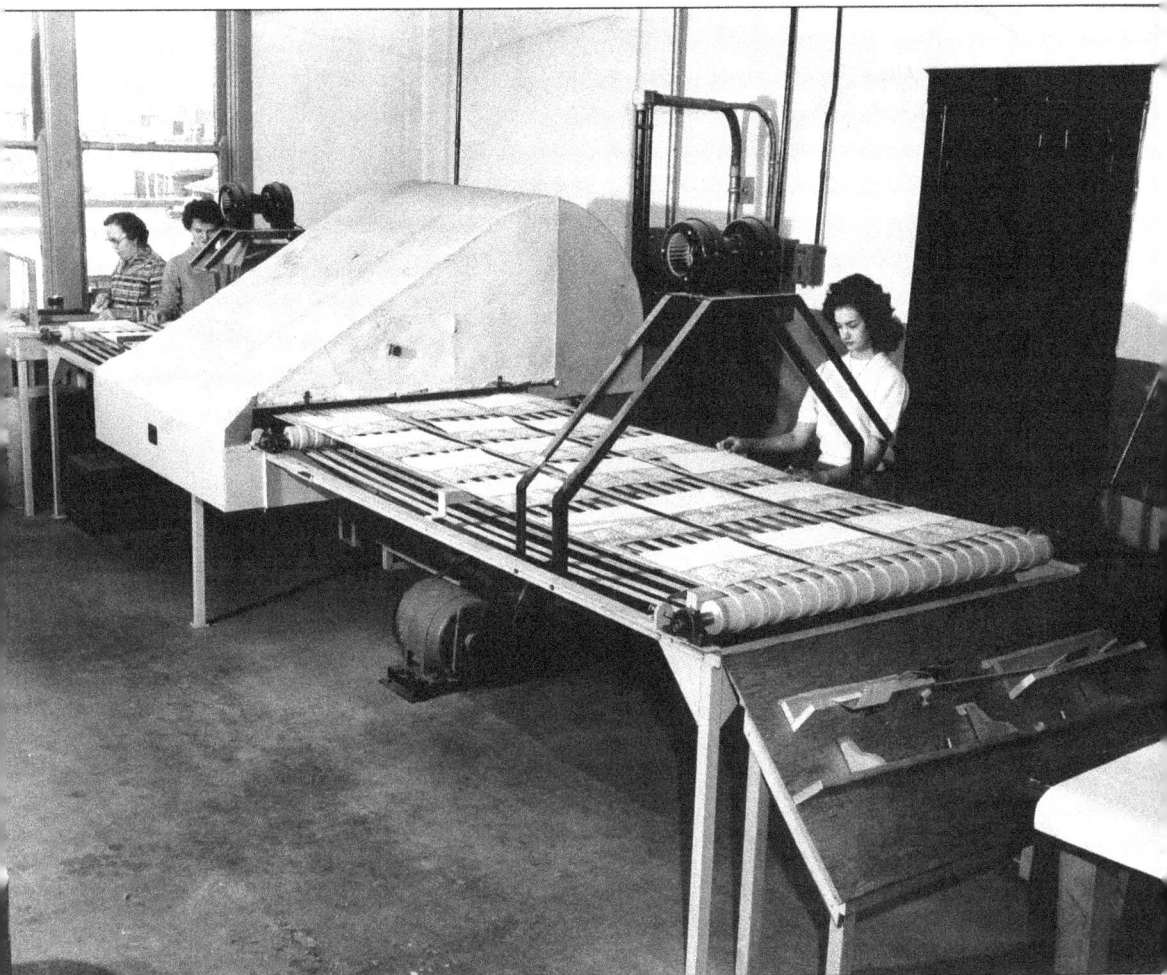

The Joliet company's silk screen adhesive dryer machine that attached and dried the glitter on the greeting cards ran in continuous operation. This machine could produce several thousand greeting cards per hour. Note the drying fan pointed down toward the cards above the woman on the right. The glitter-style card became extremely popular during the 1950s and remains popular today. (Authors' collection.)

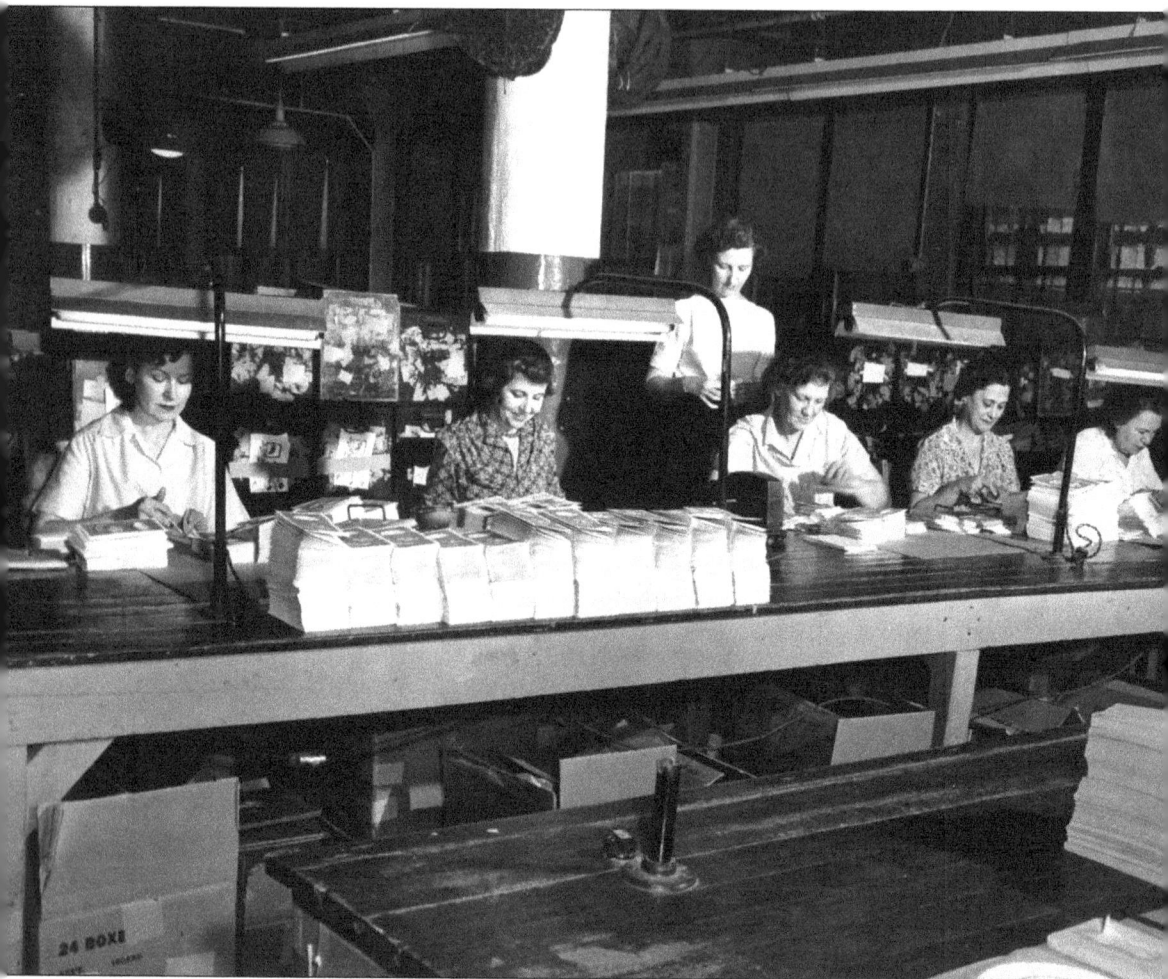

The greeting cards were stacked in front of the employees for inspection. In some cases, the cards required ribbons to be attached as well as making sure each box had an envelope included for each card. The holiday greeting line offered many opportunities for extra business for the calendar salesmen. Gerlach Barklow advertised that the businessman would "carry his message of good will into home and hearts" if he purchased its greeting cards. He would also "make his name remembered" by his customers if he sent them one of the company's greeting cards. (Authors' collection.)

On his 46th birthday, Charles C. Culp, president of the greeting card division, is seen here with several of his favorite birthday greeting cards. He is shown surrounded by original designs made by his staff artists. If he likes them, he will add them to the next year's 1952 regular line of cards. The company yearbook tells that its colorfully printed cards were made in an amazingly modern style. It also mentions the company's cards would bring back fond memories. (Authors' collection.)

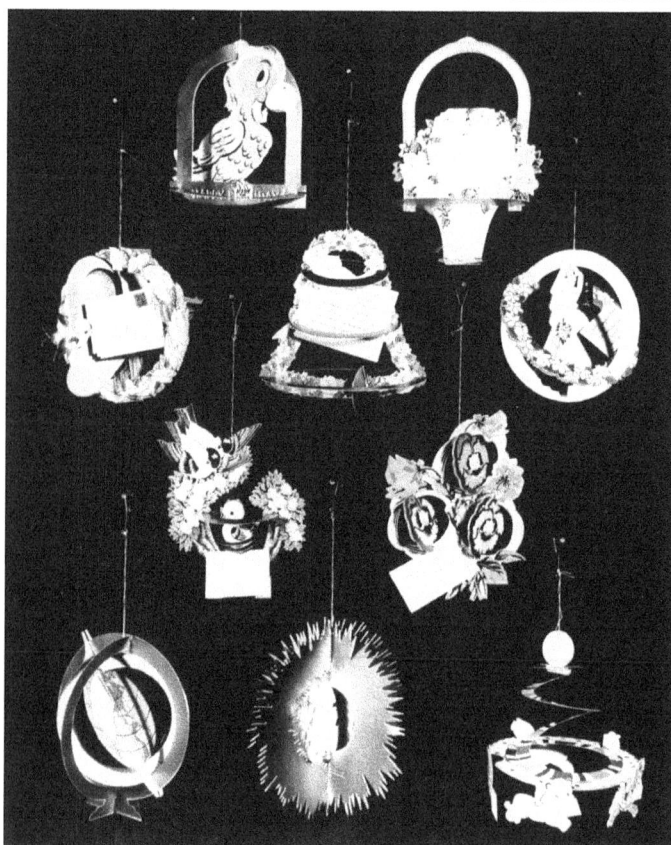

Proclaiming "I'm a bird of few words," this parrot delivers a "get well" message to Chicago model Marlene Reilly, via a newly developed Twirl-Around greeting card. In her other hand, Reilly holds a world globe card conveying the message "Congratulations and a World of Good Luck." The new three-dimensional greeting cards were introduced by the P. F. Volland Company. Pictured at left are 10 of the new Twirl-Around greeting cards, which the P. F. Volland Company also titled Color in Motion greeting cards. The product line, consisting of 26 new cards, covered such occasions as birthdays, anniversaries, and other dates. (Authors' collection.)

Two of the 1950s Christmas greeting card displays show the various cards the company offered. The friendship and convalescent cards are shown in the back on the photograph above. The boxes of cards in the photograph are marked 10 cards for 50¢. These displays were set up at the factory for potential retail store customers to come in and select their cards for the upcoming Christmas season. The display at right advertises "Now— Wide Selection, Complete Stock, Quick Printing Service." (Authors' collection.)

P. F. Volland and Rust Craft produced millions of greeting cards at the Joliet factory. The oldest known greeting card in existence is a Valentine's Day card made in the 1400s and is in a British museum. Americans began exchanging handmade Valentine's Day cards in the early 1700s. In the 1840s, Esther A. Howland began to sell the first mass-produced valentine cards. Many of the P. F. Volland and Rust Craft Valentine's Day cards had colorful pictures with ribbons or lace tied to them. (Authors' collection.)

Often the P. F. Volland wedding cards had a cartoon pictured on the front of them. Some of the greeting card artists employed at the greeting card factory also worked as artists for the large paper mills that were located in Joliet. The company also hired people who developed the sayings or greetings that were inside the cards. The greeting card companies also held contests in order to get new ideas for the front and inside of their cards. (Authors' collection.)

One former employee told about airbrushing three plates, which would go to the printers for making a greeting card. This department was on the south side of the building. She had met and married one of the pressmen. He was a pressman that she had colored the plates for during her employment. She worked at the company from 1948 through 1951. She and other employees watched from the plant's windows on May 12, 1950, as Marshall Field IV married Katherine Woodruff from Joliet at the Central Presbyterian Church on Richards Street. The groom was the great-grandson of the founder of Marshall Field and Company, and Woodruff was the daughter of a prominent Joliet family. It was said that very few cards were made at Volland that day. (Authors' collection.)

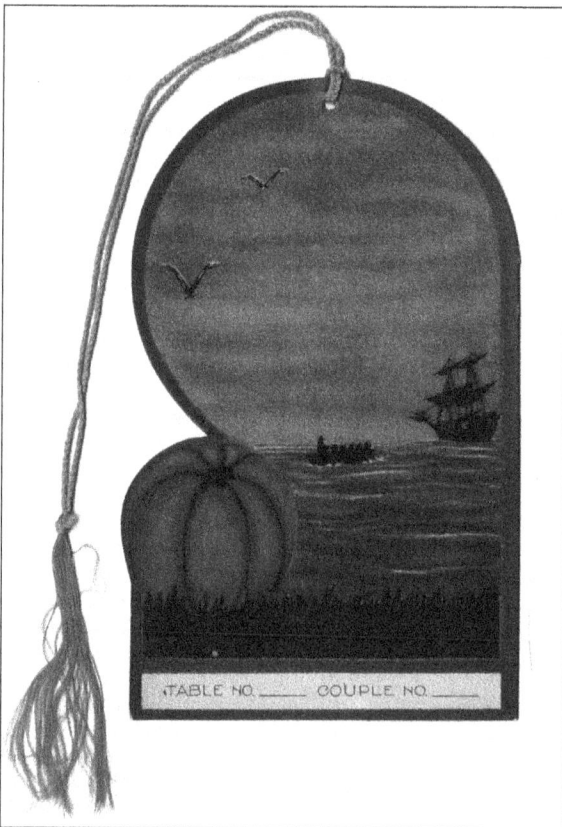

The Halloween bridge tally card above and the Halloween table setting card at left were printed by the P. F. Volland Company of Joliet. Vintage Halloween items are very collectible. Halloween postcards are by far the most sought after holiday postcards. A Halloween card with a witch or black cat printed on it can more than double the value of a card versus one with only a pumpkin pictured on it. (Authors' collection.)

The bridge and table setting cards contained images of every type of picture or holiday that comes to mind. On the front of the most popular early cards were art deco and animal images. The P. F. Volland Company reported excellent sales of bridge tally cards in the 1930s and 1940s. The bridge player's name would be printed with the score tallied on the back. (Authors' collection.)

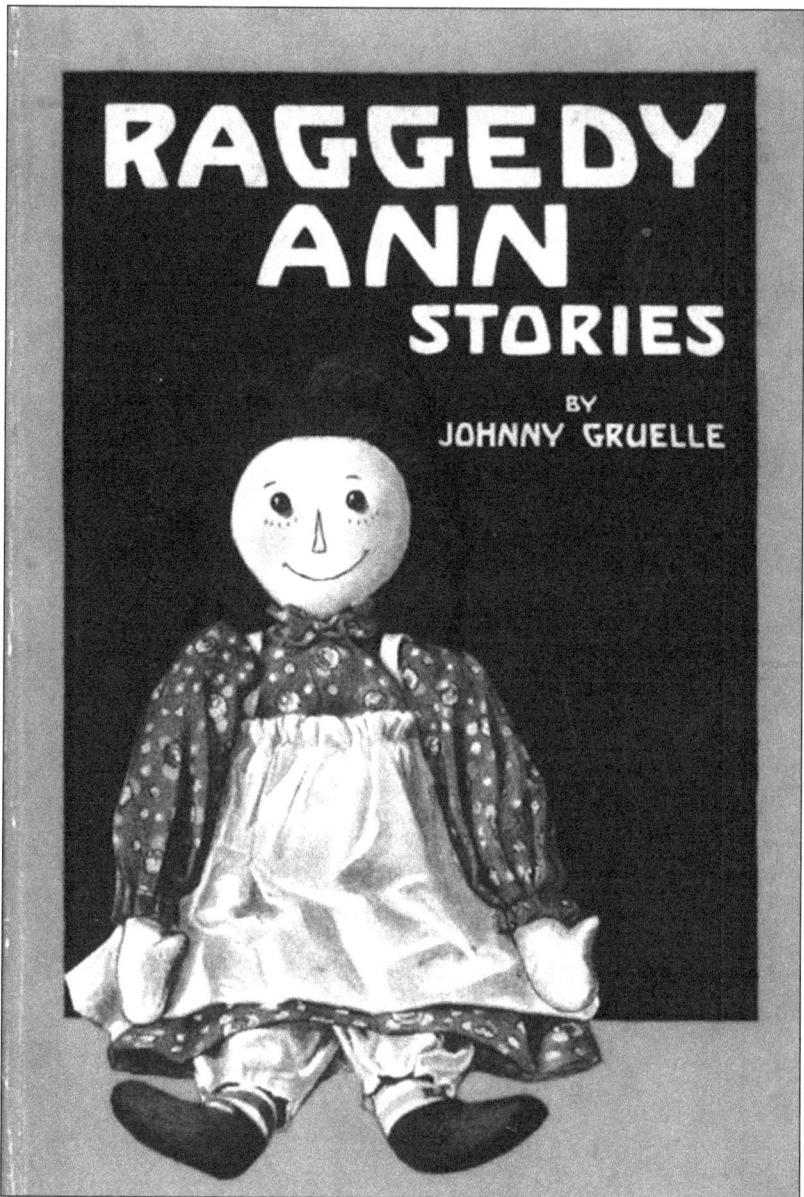

In 1918, the P. F. Volland Company began publishing the first *Raggedy Ann Stories* by Johnny Gruelle. A sequel, *Raggedy Andy Stories*, was added in 1920. The sequel introduced the character of her brother, Raggedy Andy, who was dressed in a sailor suit and hat. Gruelle was both an artist and author of children's books. He had beat out 1,500 contestants in a 1911 cartooning contest sponsored by the *New York Herald*. Prior to writing the Raggedy Ann book, Gruelle gave his ill daughter Marcella a dusty faceless doll that was found in the attic. He drew a face on the doll and named it Raggedy Ann. Gruelle's Raggedy Ann doll was patented on September 7, 1915. The first dolls were mass-produced in Connecticut. The P. F. Volland Company also manufactured some of the earlier Raggedy Ann dolls. In addition to the Raggedy Ann books, Gruelle authored and illustrated several other books. He illustrated a 1914 edition of *Grimm's Fairy Tales*. His brother Justin was also an accomplished illustration artist who painted calendar images for the Gerlach Barklow Company. Johnny Gruelle passed away in Miami Beach in 1938. (Authors' collection.)

CHICAGO
NEW YORK

BOSTON
TORONTO

THE P. F. VOLLAND COMPANY

BOOKS - MOTTOES — *PUBLISHERS* — GREETING CARDS

Manufacturers of Volland Leathercraft

WASHINGTON AND RICHARDS STREET
JOLIET, ILLINOIS

Along with several other books written by L. Frank Baum, the P. F. Volland Company also printed Baum's book *The Wizard of Oz*. His second son, Robert Stanton Baum, was married to Edna Ducker from Joliet. The Ducker family lived on Richards Street near the Gerlach Barklow and Volland factory. Edna had one of the best-preserved *The Wizard of Oz* and Baum family collections. An original edition of one of the *The Wizard of Oz* books was presented by L. Frank Baum to each of his four sons. Until her death in 1968, Edna generously made the collection available to Baum and *The Wizard of Oz* historians. (Authors' collection.)

Remember

A RECORD OF YOUR CLASS DAYS

Compiled, Edited and Illustrated By Three Girls, Marie, Ethel and Dorothy, who Themselves Kept a Record of Their School Days, and Know what You will want to Remember

Published by
THE P. F. VOLLAND COMPANY
JOLIET, ILLINOIS
NEW YORK   BOSTON

This 1927 P. F. Volland Company book printed in Joliet is titled *Remember: A Record of Your Class Days*. The P. F. Volland Company did this book for college students to document their memories during the school years. It had a page for students' first impressions on their first day at college, photographs of their roommates, sororities, favorite professors, motor parties, and favorite haunts, and mementos, and it even had a page for dance cards and favors. Volland advertised that the book was "Compiled, Edited and Illustrated by Three Girls, Marie, Ethel, and Dorothy, who Themselves Kept a Record of Their School Days, and Know what You will want to Remember." (Authors' collection.)

HIM
Pictures and descriptions

Four

Lois Delander, Joliet's Miss America 1927

The first Miss America contest was held in 1921. In 1927, Lois Delander from Joliet was crowned Miss America. Delander was 16 years old. In 1928, protesters of the Miss America pageant won out, and the pageant was discontinued. Despite the efforts of the pageant officials, the contest had gained a reputation for being too risqué. The onset of the Great Depression in 1929 did not help matters for restarting the pageant. It did not resume again until 1933. Delander won a scepter, a Bulova watch, and a screen test that she never took. At age 55, she was asked why she did not go into show business, and she stated, "I was either too busy or too tired to do so."

Delander was featured as Miss America on several Gerlach Barklow Company calendars. Both famous female Gerlach Barklow artists, Zula Kenyon and Adelaide Hiebel, did artwork of Delander for calendars. Her calendar images graced tens of thousands of calendars and were some of the most popular selling calendars by Gerlach Barklow in the late 1920s.

Delander, the daughter of a county clerk and his wife, and her family were almost overcome by the media attention of her selection as Miss America. It was reported that theatrical companies were willing to pay her $1,000 a week for stage appearances, but Delander worried about "catching up" at school. After her Miss America reign was over, Delander returned home to Joliet to finish her studies. Soft-spoken and studious, Delander is pictured in the Joliet Township High School yearbooks, graduating in 1930. She missed one year of school due to winning the contest. Crowds would gather on the weekends with people pointing at her when she would walk around the local Dellwood Park with her sister. After college, she married stockbroker Ralph Lang and raised three daughters. "I've lived happily ever after," said Delander. In 1946, at age 35, Delander weighed four pounds less than she did as Miss America. She was the grandmother of seven children and lived in a suburb of Chicago until she passed away in 1985 at age 74.

Joliet's Lois Delander was the first Miss Illinois pageant winner to become Miss America. The Miss Illinois contest was held at the Oriental Theater in Chicago. Her Miss Illinois contest prizes included a five-week vaudeville contract at $100 a week. Since her crowning, five more Miss Illinois winners have gone on to become Miss America. She was a member of the high school glee club and a student of piano and classical ballet. She had won both a musical memory contest and a medal for knowing Bible verses before becoming Miss America. She also excelled in Latin. As a surprise, her father drove out to Atlantic City only to arrive 15 minutes before she was crowned. Delander had given herself so little chance of winning that she packed her bags for departure the night before the finals. After winning and without ambitions for a film or stage career, she returned home to complete her high school studies. (Authors' collection.)

This print of Delander, titled *American Beauties*, was the artwork of Adelaide Hiebel and appeared as a Gerlach Barklow calendar. The original pastel painting still hangs in the Rialto Theatre on Chicago Street in Joliet. Joliet residents gathered in the Rialto Theatre during the contest. Within five minutes of the judges' decision, the announcement was made at the Rialto Theatre that Delander had won the contest and was to become the next Miss America. Delander also won first place in the popularity contest voted on by the other girls in the contest. Maurice Rubens, pictured below, was one of the owners of the Rialto Theatre. Delander stated in 1968, "Maurice Rubens built the new Rialto Theatre. He came to the Castle dancing school, talent scouting. Like most kids in that era, my sister Norma and I went to ballet and piano classes. Mr. Rubens and Miss Castle persuaded my parents, and me, that I enter the Miss Joliet contest." (Authors' collection.)

This rare panoramic photograph of the 1927 Miss America contestants is titled "Inter-City Beauties, Atlantic City Pageant 1927." Lois Delander, Miss Illinois, is the seventh girl from the left in the top row of this photograph. In 1927, several of the contestants were sponsored by cities versus states. In this photograph, some cities represented include Boston, Tulsa, Utica, Pontiac, Kansas City, Battle Creek, and Minneapolis. There is even a Miss Boardwalk Illustrated News pictured that was a contestant. The Native American girl in the bottom row near the middle is wearing a banner titled Miss Princess America. Many people protested these early Miss

America contests that featured bare limbs and bobbed hair. In 1921, the first contest was held as a photographic "popularity contest" from city finalists known as "Inter-City Beauties." The girl outfitted in the American flag–style dress pictured next to the man is the 1926 winner, Norma Smallwood. Smallwood had requested $600 from the pageant for her appearance to crown the 1927 winner. When the pageant official could not come up with the money forthright, she left the event to accept a paying job in North Carolina. (Authors' collection.)

Gerlach Barklow artist Zula Kenyon painted this image of Lois Delander that was used on a calendar. The title of this print is *Lois*. When Delander won the contest, the Fred Waring Orchestra played "There She Goes, Miss America." Delander did not cry or react emotionally. She stated, "I marched down the ramp as we practiced." She had received 8 of 15 votes for the finalists. The girls were not required to perform a talent. They did have to appear in a swimsuit and an evening gown. Her evening gown was an above-the-knee-length, white velvet dress with crystal bead fringe. (Authors' collection.)

The most famous pastel painting of Lois Delander is titled *Miss America* and pictures her in a swimsuit. The swimsuit worn in the contest covered a majority of her body. She wore flesh-colored leotards so as not to show her bare legs. Delander was described by the newspapers as having blue-gray eyes, peaches-and-cream complexion, weighing 120 pounds, and being five feet, four and a half inches tall. Her measurements were listed as 33-25-34, and it was noted that she had "a body of great form." This painting hung in the rotunda of the Rialto Theatre for many years before disappearing. The theater had been under renovation during the time it disappeared. Illustration art collectors and Joliet residents have not been able to locate the whereabouts of this very famous Gerlach Barklow Company Miss America pastel painting. This painting was one of the best-selling calendars in the Gerlach Barklow Company's history. (Authors' collection.)

This photograph is of Lois Delander standing next to her new home on West Acres Road in Joliet. At some point following Delander's selection as Miss America, the house was constructed. Because of the pile of dirt behind Delander, it appears that this photograph was taken during or shortly after construction of the house. It was occupied by the Delander family from 1930 to 1932 and again from 1935 to 1939. During 1933 and 1934, it was occupied by the vice president of one of the Joliet wallpaper mills. The Delander family moved to Union Street in Joliet during the 1933–1934 time frame. (Courtesy of Tony and Sandy Contos.)

Five

ZULA KENYON

Zula Kenyon was one of the most popular early female illustration artists in America and for many years was a leading artist for the Gerlach Barklow Company. She was born in 1873 in Deansville, Wisconsin. Her father, John Kenyon, was a minister. She was mostly a self-taught artist and had drawn lifelike portraits of many of her young classmates. Kenyon began attending the Art Institute of Chicago in 1899, even though women were not encouraged to attend college and start careers during this time period. At the beginning of her career, Kenyon had a studio in both Chicago and Waterloo, Wisconsin. Her favorite medium was pastels. She ground her own pastels to achieve the colors she preferred to use on her original pastel paintings.

Kenyon produced over 250 calendar images for the Gerlach Barklow Company during her career. She began at Gerlach Barklow right after the company was started in 1907. Her early work is signed only as Kenyon, due to the fact that many male customers had reservations about purchasing calendars painted by a female artist. Kenyon soon became one of the Gerlach Barklow Company's best-selling artists, and she was hired with an exclusive contract. She was very well known for her subjects being a beautiful woman holding a bouquet of flowers, as well as for the famous calendar line of little girls with a bluebird. Edward J. Barklow had the idea of creating a "Bluebird of Happiness" theme. He suggested the idea to Kenyon after seeing a stage performance of Maurice Maeterlinck's *The Blue Bird*. She completed the first Bluebird series subject, titled *The Song of the Bluebird*, for the 1926 calendar line. The Bluebird series ran for the next 30-plus years and proved to be the most popular Gerlach Barklow Company calendar line ever produced.

By 1918, Kenyon's health had become poor, and she moved to Arizona, eventually settling in California. Kenyon continued to produce calendar art for the Gerlach Barklow Company, with her last published work being a Bluebird series print that appeared in the 1939 calendar line. Kenyon passed away in 1947.

This image by Zula Kenyon, titled *The Song of the Bluebird*, was the first in a long-running Bluebird series by the Gerlach Barklow Company. Kenyon would go on to paint eight of the Bluebird series girls, with her last being in 1939. Keeping with a series like the Bluebird calendar series year after year was a marketing strategy by the Gerlach Barklow Company. If a local dairy gave away a Bluebird series calendar each year, the customers would be standing in line to see what the next "Bluebird girl" image would be on the next year's dairy calendar. The previous year's calendar image would be cut out, framed, and hung on the customer's wall. This was a very common practice for the customers to do, especially during the Depression years when people could not afford to buy pictures for their homes. This is the reason so many of these early calendar prints survived for all those years. This calendar also had an image of the bank at the bottom, along with a listing of the officers of the bank. (Authors' collection.)

Kenyon was best known for her artwork of beautiful young women holding a bouquet of flowers. This is an excellent example that is titled *My Luv's Like a Red, Red Rose*. It was copyrighted in 1914 and used in the Gerlach Barklow calendar line in 1916. The original pastel painting of this image is one of the few known original pastels by Kenyon that still exists. It is not known what happened to the over 250 original pastel paintings created by Kenyon. The original illustration artwork was not thought of as artwork or collectible, such as fine art was in the early 20th century. It is possible that many of the original paintings may have been destroyed or thrown away. It was documented by some calendar companies that they destroyed the original artwork rather than sell it. This was done so it would not fall into the hands of their competitors. There is no evidence that the Gerlach Barklow Company destroyed any of its artwork. According to a 1911 Gerlach Barklow booklet, there was even a gallery at the company in Joliet where original artwork could be purchased. (Authors' collection.)

LILLIAN ANDERSON CORSET SHOP

1614 Heyworth Building
29 E. Madison St., CHICAGO

Telephone Central 289

Often only one or two known prints exist of a Zula Kenyon calendar image. This 1914 calendar has one of the very rare images by Kenyon. It advertises Lillian Anderson Corset Shop on Madison Street in Chicago. Such prints are sought after by illustration collectors across the United States. Collectors often try to have one print or calendar of every image by a certain artist such as Kenyon in their collection. The hard-to-find images by an artist such as Zula Kenyon are more valuable to the collectors. The image at left has not been found with a title on the print. Often the prints were not titled on the print by the calendar company. This makes these prints even harder to find when searching on the Internet. (Authors' collection.)

Kenyon also provided artwork that was used on hand fans made of light cardboard. Air-conditioning did not exist, and these fans were very popular in the early 20th century. The Gerlach Barklow Company would put a beautiful young woman by Kenyon on one side of the fan and a company's advertisement on the opposite side. These fans were sometimes called funeral fans since funeral homes would hand them out during services. This fan advertises a hardware, harness, furniture, and undertaking business on the back. Very often, the furniture maker was also the undertaker. This was largely due to the fact that they could make the wooden caskets as well as furniture. (Authors' collection.)

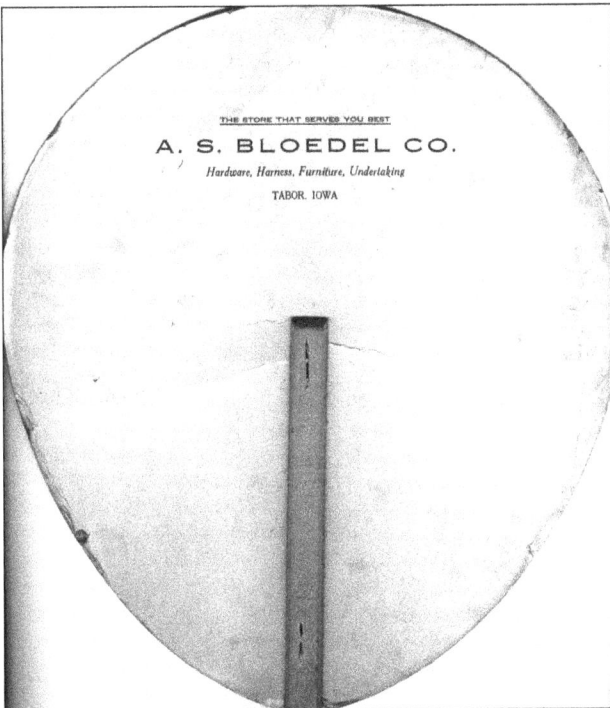

THE STORE THAT SERVES YOU BEST

A. S. BLOEDEL CO.

Hardware, Harness, Furniture, Undertaking

TABOR, IOWA

PHONES {CHICAGO 846
N. W. 1070

JOEL PETERSON
GROCERIES
FRUITS AND VEGETABLES IN SEASON
1302 JACKSON ST.   JOLIET, ILLINOIS

1915		January			1915	
SUN	MON	TUES	WED	THUR	FRI	SAT
Full Moon 1st Sun	Last Quar. 8th	New Moon 15th	First Quar. 22th		1	2
3	4	5	6	7	8	9
10	11	12	13	14	15	16
17	18	19	20	21	22	23
24/31	25	26	27	28	29	30

This 1915 calendar is from Joel Peterson Groceries located on Jackson Street in Joliet. It advertises "fruits and vegetables in season." This calendar would be considered a double collectible since it has both a Zula Kenyon image as a print, and it has Joliet advertising on it. Some collectors would want it in their collection for the Kenyon image, which is titled *Virginia*, while the Joliet collectors would buy it because it advertises a Joliet business. If it had a gas station advertisement on it such as Standard Oil from Joliet, it would be considered a triple collectible. The Standard Oil collectors would be interested in owning it, as would the Joliet and Zula Kenyon collectors. This has made collecting calendars with advertising and these great images by illustrators such as Kenyon very popular. (Authors' collection.)

Kenyon produced several postcard images for the Gerlach Barklow Company. The company produced both a dog and a cat series of postcards by her. Many of these images include a 07 after her signature, which indicates she painted the image for these postcards in 1907. This was very early in her employment at the company. The postcard craze that entranced America had started in those years beginning around 1907. The Gerlach Barklow Company was in its infancy during those years and quickly began producing postcards by the tens of thousands. (Authors' collection.)

Calendar images with a pretty woman and animals were very popular with customers in the early to middle 1900s. *Kentucky Belles* was one of these images by Zula Kenyon. It was used on this March 1913 calendar advertising Hanover Fire Insurance Company. The calendar below from the same Gerlach Barklow series and year for November, titled *Friends*, is another great example of using a pretty woman and an animal as an image. The large majority of the business's customers were men, and its Gerlach Barklow calendar products were marketed toward this clientele. These images with women and horses or dogs remain very desirable today for the calendar collectors and generally sell for more than most calendar images from this time period. (Authors' collection.)

Airplanes and aviation were gaining popularity during the 1920s after World War II. This calendar image, titled *There He Goes*, by Kenyon really touched on this market. This calendar came with a story about the print, which included, "Somewhere on the far distant horizon of this beautifully painted picture there floats a tiny speck of an airplane, and this lovely girl, with deep violet eyes shining and face wreathed in an adoring smile, is watching it. Zula Kenyon has depicted in the exquisite sweetly smiling face of this young girl a love and adoration which is inspiring to see. She has always given her portraits of a young girl in touch with beauty, but in "There He Goes" is so full of feminine ingenuousness and sweetness that we are sure she will be an unending source of delight and happiness to you. May she bring added charm and pleasure to every moment she is with you." (Authors' collection.)

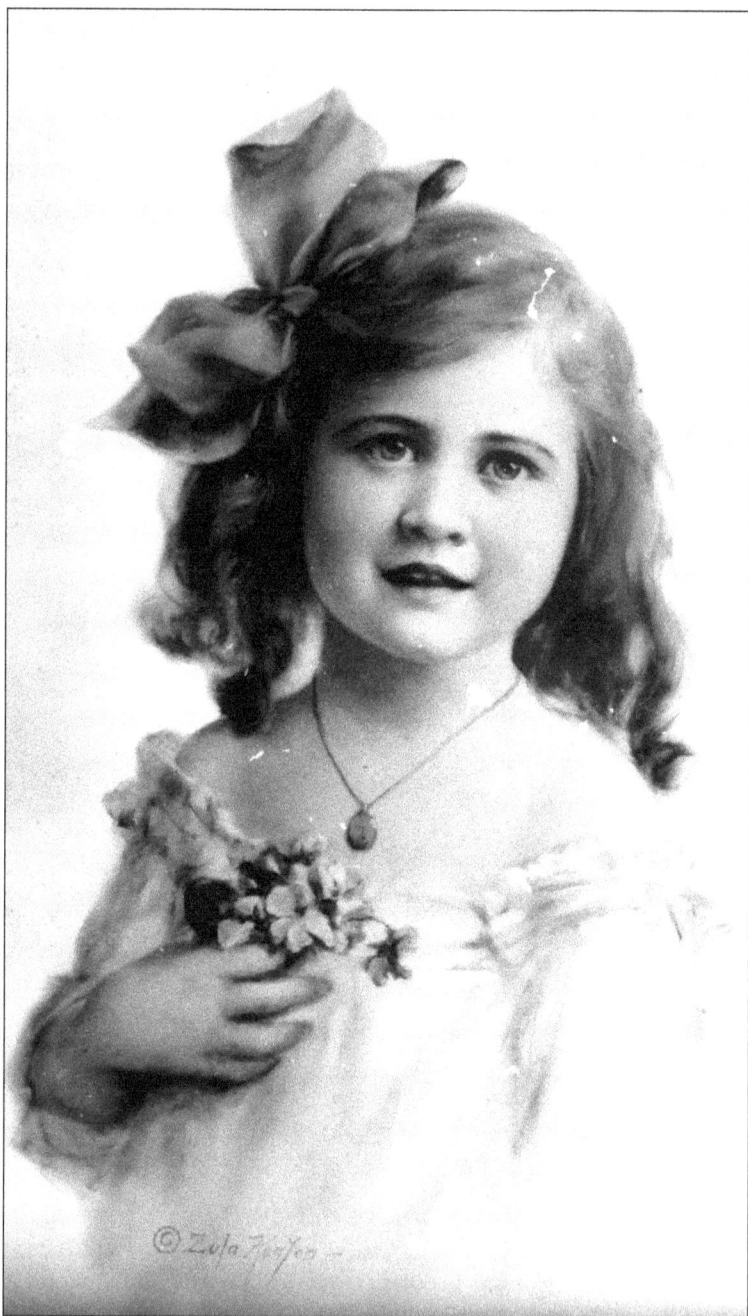

Zula Kenyon did very few children calendar images outside of the Bluebird series. The image above of a young girl holding flowers is one of Kenyon's hardest-to-find prints. These early prints were hand tinted by factory workers, and no two are exactly the same. Some art collectors feel that Kenyon had trouble illustrating hands correctly. The girl's hand in this image could be used an example of this problem. Several of her images depicting a woman holding flowers have the hands hidden from view. One story is told that she would look for a woman working in the factory that had pretty hands, and she would use her hands as a model for her painting. (Authors' collection.)

According to the *Waterloo Democrat* newspaper, in 1915, Kenyon visited Waterloo, Wisconsin, to attend some homecoming events. Waterloo was five miles from her hometown of Deansville. She had moved to Chicago in 1896. It is believed that Kenyon once had an art studio on North Madison Street in the Bibow or R. B. Togs buildings in Waterloo. Almost as soon as she moved out West from Joliet, the calendar company was advertising Kenyon as a western artist. The 1920 salesman sample book describes one of the images as a "beautiful study that is a typical example of the work of Zula Kenyon, a western artist whose pastels for richness of coloring, perfection of drawing and beauty of conception, are unsurpassed by any other artist in the world." (Authors' collection.)

Zula Kenyon was as beautiful as many of the girls that modeled for her paintings. This photograph is from a Reedsburg, Wisconsin, studio. It is one of the few photographs of her that still exists. Kenyon left Joliet and moved out West around 1918. The 1920 census lists Kenyon and her sister Haidee as living in Tucson. In this census, Zula and Haidee are listing their ages as much younger than their true ages. Zula is listed as 36 years old; however, she was born in 1873. Haidee is listed as 33 years old, even though she had been born in 1876. Sometime after 1930, the sisters moved to California. The sisters won an award for their beautiful flower gardens while living in San Diego. In 1934, the Joliet newspaper printed an article that described Zula's flower gardens in California. Zula never married. (Courtesy of Rick and Charlotte Martin.)

Six

ADELAIDE HIEBEL

Adelaide Hiebel was born in New Hope, Wisconsin, in 1886. Her father was a prominent tailor in Waterloo, and she became an expert seamstress. At an early age, she began modeling figures from clay and sketching images at Sunday school. By 11 years old, she was given a box of pastels and fell in love with this medium. Her use and talent in pastels continued for her entire career.

Hiebel's health was said to be frail during her school years. She was encouraged by both her teachers and mother to obtain formal art training. Hiebel attended a few semesters at the Art Institute of Chicago. She opened a studio in Waterloo and met Zula Kenyon, an already successful illustration artist from the area. Kenyon became Hiebel's mentor. In 1917–1919, Kenyon was working at the Gerlach Barklow Company, and her own health was forcing her to semiretire and move out West. She recommended to Theodore R. Gerlach that her good friend Adelaide Hiebel be her replacement. Gerlach sent for Hiebel, and she moved to Joliet. Hiebel began working in the studio on top of the Gerlach Barklow building, spending a few months working with Kenyon in order to learn more about Kenyon's techniques. Her early work and style was very much like that of Kenyon's artwork. In order to retain the customers that had been purchasing calendars created by Kenyon, the calendar company wanted Hiebel's early work to look very similar to the work of Kenyon.

Hiebel eventually moved her studio to her home in Joliet. She continued as a leading artist at Gerlach Barklow for over 35 years. Her artistic range was excellent, completing paintings of children, beautiful women, animals, and landscapes. Her Indian maiden subjects are highly collectible and thought by many to be some of her best work.

She made her home on John Street and later in an apartment building on Raynor Avenue in Joliet. After retiring from Gerlach Barklow in the mid-1950s, Hiebel moved to California. She had purchased several of her original pieces of artwork and moved them with her. Adelaide Hiebel passed away in 1965 in Santa Ana, California.

MISS ADELAIDE HIEBEL

Adelaide Hiebel once commented that the camera was not very friendly to her and felt she was not a pretty woman. This Gerlach Barklow Company photograph is taken from the Gerlach Barklow yearbook. It lists her as an exclusive Gerlach Barklow artist. Other exclusive artists listed include Fletcher Ransom, Zula Kenyon, and Harold S. Hewlett. An early salesman sample book showed her completing the painting titled *My Dream Girl*. She is shown painting a live model. The salesman yearbook takes the customer through a step-by-step process, beginning with Hiebel creating this painting through the entire printing procedure of the *My Dream Girl* calendar prints. (Authors' collection.)

This photograph of Hiebel appears on a 1947 calendar that pictures three cocker spaniel dogs. The title of the print is *Tom, Dick and Harry*. The story with this calendar states, "The picture 'Tom, Dick and Harry' is a reproduction of an original painting by Adelaide Hiebel, a versatile artist who specializes in human-interest subjects. Although the lively cockers could not be kept still long enough to pose for this portrait, this is really a painting from life, for Miss Hiebel faithfully followed a photograph." (Authors' collection.)

Adelaide Hiebel's early work closely resembles her mentor Zula Kenyon's work. This print, titled *Bloom of Youth*, was in the 1933 calendar line. The salesman sample booklet states, "The artist here presents a charming example of blooming youth of today. She may not be more vigorous, more athletic, and certainly healthier then sisters of a past generation, but she also has virtues of which the poet sings, and she shines the pride of those days, and will be a bright example of succeeding times. Prepared in calendar form for our friends and presented with sincere good wishes." The company produced a short article similar to this for each calendar print example in the salesman sample books. These booklets were called title leaves. (Authors' collection.)

The image *A Maiden Fair* by Hiebel was copyrighted in 1924. The Gerlach Barklow Company yearbook stated, "A calendar is a MUST in ANY modern home. It is just as much a part of that home as any other piece of furniture or furnishing. It is looked at more than any other one thing in the home, for obviously hung in a conspicuous place at or near eye level." (Authors' collection.)

Often the calendar image titles would be used more than once by Gerlach Barklow. This 1938 calendar painting by Adelaide Hiebel is titled *My Luve's Like a Red, Red Rose.* This same title was also used on a Zula Kenyon image only *Luve's* was spelled *Luv's.* That year, Gerlach Barklow told its salesmen, "Each sales person for the first ten weeks of the new year should set their mark at not less than $100 a day of sales—and then beat that mark, and not just occasionally, but every day—six days a week. Veterans, of course should set their mark higher than this, but this is a fair mark for a new salesman." This implies that the salesmen were expected to work six days per week. (Authors' collection.)

Hiebel's Bluebird series images appeared in at least 20 Gerlach Barklow calendars. The 1940 yearbook states, "The 'Bluebird' calendar is a trademark of a thousand businesses. The continuity and freshness are fundamental of resultful calendar advertising. Buyers recognize the calendar and identify with the sponsor even before they read the imprint." The Bluebird calendar girls were often local Joliet children who were picked to model for the calendars. One Bluebird series girl told that she was given a Raggedy Ann doll and her parents paid $5 for allowing her to model. Gerlach Barklow advertisements read that the Bluebird series was its oldest and most famous follow-up subject. The advertisement stated, "It is used by businessmen in all parts of the country, and helps them sell everything from machinery to life insurance and real estate." (Authors' collection.)

Safely Guarded

Adelaide Hiebel's ability to paint children images was well known throughout the calendar industry. The calendar company ran a campaign for several years, titled Safety First or Safety Series, with Hiebel's images. The campaign marketed that no topic was more important to America than traffic safety. It reminded its audience of "safety first." Pedestrians were warned to cross streets carefully, and drivers were urged to protect children. Gerlach Barklow advertised that the campaign would win recognition for the businessman, due to his public-spirited advertising, and that most schools would be happy to hang Safety First calendars in their classrooms. (Authors' collection.)

THE SAFETY LESSON

SAFETY SUE
and HER FRIENDS

The Gerlach Barklow Company also sold Safety First booklets that detailed traffic and pedestrian safety. All of these booklets were illustrated with Adelaide Hiebel's children images. One of the booklets was titled *Safety Sue*, which was geared toward young girls, while another booklet directed toward boys was titled *Safety Steve*. The booklets contained advertising on the back cover for the company sponsoring the printing. (Authors' collection.)

Presented by

EXCHANGE SAVINGS BANK

"There's Safety in Savings"

MT. PLEASANT, MICHIGAN

•

Member of F. D. I. C.
Member of Federal Reserve System

◆

Always Be Careful:
The Folks at Home
Await Your Safe Return

The Buckaroo image by Adelaide Hiebel was so popular in the 1930s that the company also featured it in the 1952 calendar line. The salesman sample book described this image as follows: "Typical of the nattily attired young straight-shooter who preserves law and order in nurseries, living rooms, backyards and playgrounds in every corner of the nation is 'The Buckaroo,' portrayed in clear-eyed pursuit of duty by noted artist Adelaide Hiebel. She does her best work in depicting contemporary American children. Busy as he is in bringing in cattle rustlers and bandits to justice, the buckaroo always can find time for a friendly word, as he reins in his mount to say 'Howdy Folks.'" (Authors' collection.)

The Indian maidens by Adelaide Hiebel are considered by many art collectors as her best works. Between 1905 and 1945, Indian maiden images appeared in almost every type of advertising in America. Often these calendar images were beautiful Caucasian girls dressed as Native Americans, wearing a Native American headband, beads, and a costume. The American public adored these Indian maiden girls for several years, until the 1940s World War II–era pinup girls surpassed them in popularity. Often the Indian maiden was pictured with an animal, such as in the print below, titled *In a Forrest Glade*. Seldom would a Native American brave appear with the Native American girl, as in the image to the right, titled *Indian Love Call*. (Authors' collection.)

This Indian maiden image was used on calendar prints, a German magazine titled the *Die Hausfrau*, and even a jigsaw puzzle. Adelaide Hiebel's original pastels of these Indian maidens, as well as many of her original works, were very large at 30 inches by 40 inches. They were all on canvas. This image has been seen both titled *Fire-Fly* and *Wah-Wah-Taysee*. Hiebel did several Indian maidens during her career and actually purchased one of them for herself that was titled *In the Heart of the Lily*. Unlike many of her peers, she owned several of her original illustration pastels. She purchased them from the calendar company after they were no longer being used by the company. It is not known what happened to the paintings she owned after her death in California in the mid-1960s. (Authors' collection.)

Seven

ADDITIONAL GERLACH BARKLOW ARTISTS AND THEIR CALENDAR IMAGES

The Gerlach Barklow Company employed various artists to produce different images to maintain the appeal and reach out to individual businesses, depending on what product they were advertising. A local dairy may have wanted to utilize young children images on its calendars, while a gas station and automobile repair garage found that a pretty girl or pinup print on its calendars would lead to repeat customers.

The Gerlach Barklow Company employed a few artists that it considered "Exclusive G-B Artists," such as Zula Kenyon, Adelaide Hiebel, Fletcher Ransom, and Harold S. Hewlett. In addition, the company used artwork from several hundred artists over the decades it was in business. All the artists normally had a specialty, whether it was images of pretty girls, pinups, children, sports, outdoors themes, or landscapes. The calendar company would request a specific type of image from these artists that it felt would sell well to its customers. The company would continue to buy an artist's work year after year if it sold well. If it was selling well, the company would use follow-up subjects that had similar images year after year, such as the Bluebird series. Often the Gerlach Barklow Company would request these images. Each year, a new image would come along. It would be a fresh image, but it still would feature the child and bluebird, which would become a trademark for the customer. This marketing approach helped ensure repeat business for both the calendar company and the customer and also promised repeat work for the illustration artist.

Even though they produced great illustrations that appeared on tens of thousands of calendars and magazines, illustration artists were not recognized by the art critics. The paintings and popular images that these illustration artists completed were considered more commercial and were snubbed by the art world. After many years of being overlooked, this artwork began to gain recognition. Illustration art has become very popular with art collectors and museums that had previously not accepted it.

THE SUNSHINE GIRL

©THE GERLACH-BARKLOW CO
JOLIET, ILL.

Rolf Armstrong was born in Bay City, Michigan, in 1899. He later studied at the Art Institute of Chicago. He produced a few images for the Gerlach Barklow Company. His original glamour girl artwork has become some of the most collectible and valuable illustrations. He refused to work from photographs and always used live models. In the 1940s, he met a stunning young woman named Jewel Flowers whom he deemed as the "perfect, dream come true model." Armstrong did not sell any of his images of Jewel Flowers to Gerlach Barklow. However, she graced the calendars of other companies for almost 20 years. Armstrong produced images for several magazine covers during his career, as well as many pieces of sheet music. Armstrong passed away on February 22, 1960, in Hawaii. (Authors' collection.)

The Charlotte Becker print above is titled *Hi* and was in the 1951 calendar line. The company wrote, "Born in Dresden, Miss Becker came to America when she was a small child. From her earliest school days she adorned the margins of her school books and papers with pictures of babies. Her sketches were so good that teachers reprimanded her with reluctance. Today Miss Becker stands in the forefront of her profession. It is our sincere hope that you may have as much pleasure receiving this picture as we have presenting it to you." Becker produced dozens of images of children over many years for the Gerlach Barklow Company calendar lines. (Authors' collection.)

This image by Haskell Coffin is titled *Violets Bring Thoughts of You* and was in the 1930 Gerlach Barklow Company calendar line. Gerlach Barklow mentioned in 1930 that "we hope that the girl pictured here in such glowing loveliness will add many pleasant moments to your day and the calendar which she adorns will serve you most usefully." (Authors' collection.)

Coffin was best known for his images of beautiful women. His second marriage was to Francis Starr, a well-known actress who often modeled for her husband. This Gerlach Barklow calendar image, titled *Molly*, is typical of Coffin's soft delicate pastels featuring young, pretty women. The 1931 Gerlach Barklow advertisement for this print and its model read, in part, "We trust she may add a little bit of sunshine and happiness to every hour she is with you." (Authors' collection.)

Bradshaw Crandell was born in 1896 and passed away in 1966. He studied at Wesleyan University and the Art Institute of Chicago. *Cosmopolitan* magazine featured his artwork on the cover for many years. He also did magazine covers for the *Saturday Evening Post*, *Collier's*, and *Redbook* magazines, in addition to painting images for the Gerlach Barklow calendars for several years. Crandell was reported to be one of the highest-paid illustrators of his time. (Authors' collection.)

Many of Crandell's images for the Gerlach Barklow calendars were pinups. The company used several Crandell paintings as a follow-up subject, titled Feathered Friends. The company stated, "Polly plays a part by giving Crandell subjects personality." In 1931, Gerlach Barklow requested Bradshaw Crandell paint an unusual pretty girl subject holding a parrot. The parrot gave the calendar print a touch of added interest that made it stand out among other pretty girl images. (Authors' collection.)

Francis (James Francis) Day was born in Leroy, New York, in 1863 and began his studies of art at the Art Students League in New York. Later he studied in Paris under famous teachers at the École des Beaux-Arts. After returning from France, he opened a studio in Berkshire, Massachusetts. A member of the National Academy, Day was famed for his portraits and child studies. This 1934 image, titled *The Rehearsal*, like all of his work, displays that delicacy and poetic charm for which he is noted. (Authors' collection.)

Edward M. Eggleston did a few images for the Gerlach Barklow Company, including this one from the 1940 title leaves salesman sample book. The salesman sample book states, "Edward M. Eggleston, the artist to whom we are indebted for this lovely portrait, was born in Ashtabula, Ohio. He received his art training at the Columbus Art School. His first practical experience was in the field of stained glass designing. He later opened a studio for general commercial art work. Eventually he found his way to New York City, where he specializes in feminine figures and storytelling pictures for which he has become eminently successful." This Gerlach Barklow print is titled *A Bonnie Lassie*. Eggleston is best known for his images of Indian maidens, pirate girls, and bathing girls in swimsuits, as well as Peter Pan images. Eggleston passed away in 1941. (Authors' collection.)

TWIN CITY HARDWARE

Floyd Scharfenberg, Proprietor

PHONE 2-9405

707 West Chestnut Street   Bloomington, Illinois

JANUARY · 1954

Jules Erbit did over 50 images for the Gerlach Barklow Company during his career. He was born in Budapest and studied in Munich. Erbit came to America in 1930. He had five daughters and lived in New York City. He always worked with pastels, and often his paintings were very large. Most of his images were of wholesome girls; however, he did produce several nude images that were used on calendars. He also did several images for Palmolive soap advertisements. His glamour girl and original pastels sell for much less than some of the better-known illustrators. In recent years, his work has gained some popularity with illustration collectors. (Authors' collection.)

Pearl Frush is considered one of the top female glamour girl calendar artists. She studied at the Art Institute of Chicago and opened her first studio in Chicago in the 1940s. She was one of Gerlach Barklow's premium and best-selling artists during 1940s and 1950s. This image, titled *Forever Yours*, is an excellent example of one of her best works that shows her exceptional talent as an illustration artist. She created much of her glamour girl artwork with pastels. (Authors' collection.)

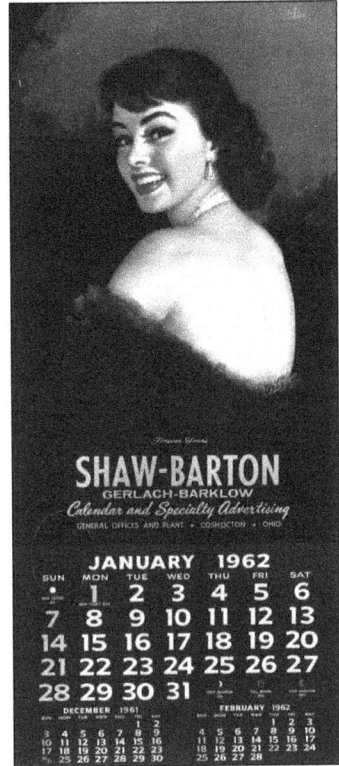

SHAW-BARTON
GERLACH-BARKLOW
Calendar and Specialty Advertising
GENERAL OFFICES AND PLANT · COSHOCTON · OHIO

		JANUARY		**1962**		
SUN	MON	TUE	WED	THU	FRI	SAT
	1	2	3	4	5	6
7	8	9	10	11	12	13
14	15	16	17	18	19	20
21	22	23	24	25	26	27
28	29	30	31			

HAPPY LANDING

Frush did several successful Gerlach Barklow glamour girl series images. Almost all her work is signed only with her last name, Frush. Occasionally some of her Gerlach Barklow work is signed Pearl Frush Brudon. Brudon was her married name. It has been speculated that a woman producing glamour girl and pinup paintings may have been requested by the calendar company to sign her work only with her last name. This would have been done to hide the fact that the artist was a woman. (Authors' collection.)

115

Goddard was a pseudonym used by two artists, Mrs. L. G. Woolfenden and Rudolph Ingerle. Woolfenden specialized in photography, while Ingerle was an artist who studied at the Art Institute of Chicago. They combined their skills to produce calendar images. Woolfenden would take photographs of models and hand color and cut out the images. She would then apply them to a canvas, and Ingerle would paint in the background, blending it with the photograph that had been attached to the canvas. Often people viewing this original artwork do not realize part of the painting is actually a photograph. (Authors' collection.)

In his painting *Sunrise*, Harold S. Hewlett presents a scene of unusual color and beauty. Hewlett was the art director at Gerlach Barklow for many years, as well as being a leading illustrator for the company. The 1942 salesman sample booklet states, "Few painters know such scenes as this first hand, as does H.S. Hewlett, who as a boy, often tramped ten miles before sunrise with an old muzzle loading gun on his shoulder. He was never able to bag more than two ducks, but his early morning expeditions brought out an innate love of nature which through the magic of his brush, he is able to portray for our enjoyment." Hewlett lived in Plainfield. His home overlooked a lake that was very similar to the one pictured in the print. (Authors' collection.)

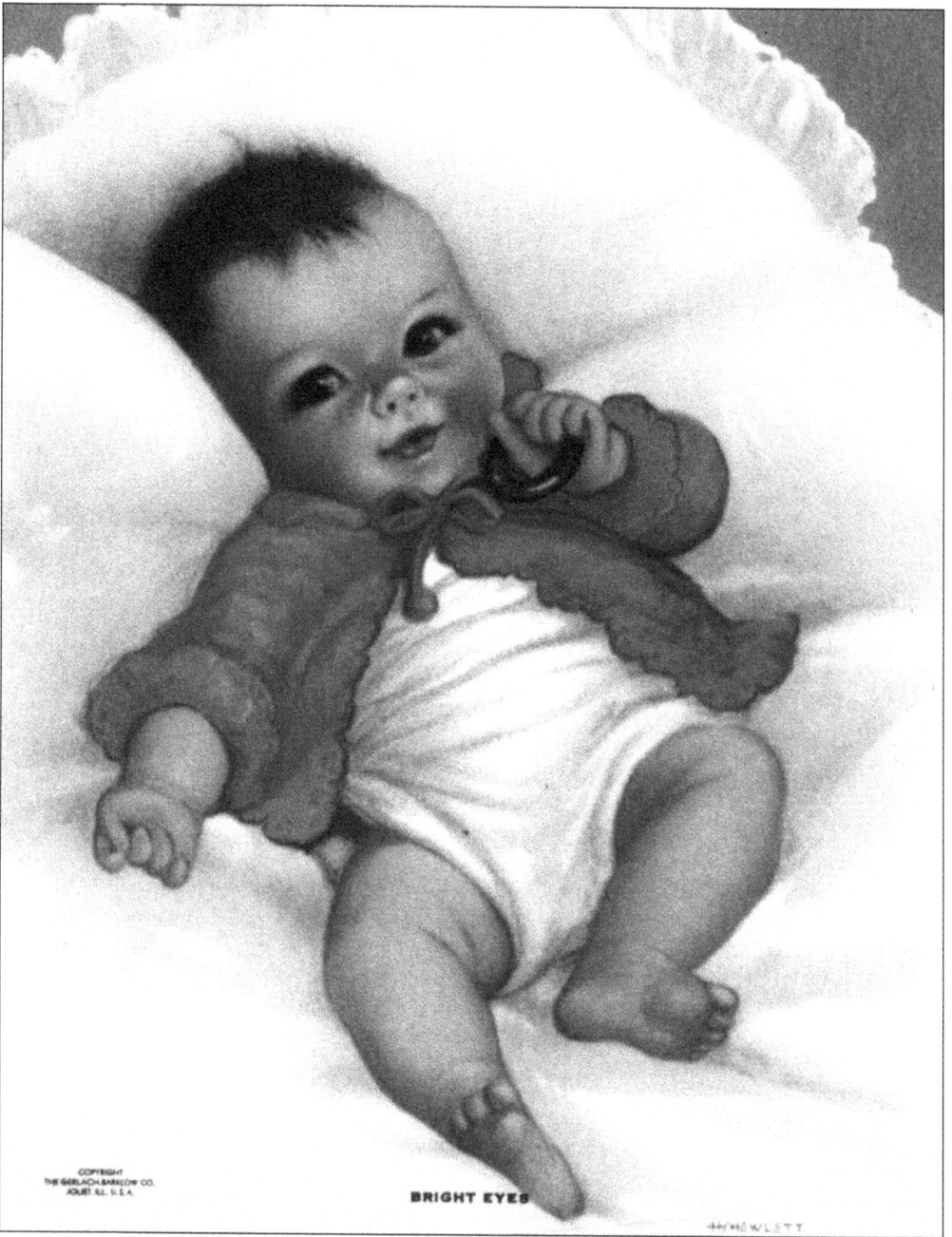

This image of the 1941 calendar line is titled *Bright Eyes* and was painted by Harold S. Hewlett. A description of this image said that "Bright Eyes isn't really my name, but folks call me that and ask me where I got the bright eyes, and a lot of other questions I can't answer. This is such a wonderful world and there is so much to see and learn, and then, too, I have to grow. So, I just eat and sleep, play and laugh—and sometimes cry—but someday I'll be a grown up. H.S. Hewlett is a versatile mid-west artist. He knows children, having a charming family of his own, reared in a pleasant suburban Illinois town." (Authors' collection.)

Hy Hintermeister was actually a father-and-son team that worked under that name. They were actually John Henry Hintermeister, who was born in 1870, and his son Henry, who was born in 1897. John was born in Switzerland and came to the United States in his early 20s. He had studied at the Zurich Museum of Art School. His son Henry studied at the Art Students League of New York. The father-and-son team painted illustrations for many years. They worked as a team, both signing the works as Hy Hintermeister. The father completed the early illustration paintings. Henry worked on several of the paintings with his father for years until John's death in 1945. After his father's death, Henry completed calendar paintings into the 1960s under the Hy Hintermeister name. Henry died in 1970. They did several works for the Gerlach Barklow Company, and their artwork has become very collectible. Many of their images depict humorous happenings. (Authors' collection.)

Ole Larsen painted this great calendar image for the 1953 Gerlach Barklow calendar line. It is titled *Field Day*. Larsen attended a retrieving school when he noticed an English setter by the name of Happy Jim. Larsen stated that "he was posed on point on liberated birds for my paintings and I was very impressed with his willingness to retrieve." Gerlach Barklow advertised that "because Happy Jim has a great future before him, we feel his picture is appropriate to welcome the New Year and wish you the best of everything in the days ahead. With this useful calendar we send a message of sincere appreciation." Calendars with outdoor scenes had great appeal to many of the company's customers. (Authors' collection.)

Irene Patten shared a studio with her sister Laurette in Chicago. Both sisters were well-known calendar illustrators. The image below by Irene is titled *Somebody's Sweetheart*, while the image to the right is titled *In Clover*. These images were both in the 1934 Gerlach Barklow calendar line. The Gerlach Barklow Company wrote, "We hope the artist's conception of "Somebody's Sweetheart" will find a place in your heart, as well as your wall." Irene produced a diverse range of images from children with animals to risqué women. Very little is known of Irene, which is typical of a majority of the early illustrators. (Authors' collection.)

Gene Pressler was born in Jersey City, New Jersey. His "Cleopatra girl" images, like this 1932 Gerlach Barklow calendar image titled *Daughter of the Nile*, are gorgeous. He always did his works in chalk pastels. He did several illustrations for Pompeian beauty cream advertisements. The advertisement for the *Daughter of the Nile* calendar states, "Moonlight, waving palms and rippling water of a softly flowing river form a suitable setting for this comely maiden of the land and time of Cleopatra. So fair is she that she might be that famous queen herself. The artist created a picture of rare grace and beauty." In a 1932 booklet, the Gerlach Barklow Company told its salesmen to "familiarize yourself with the story ad that goes with each image for 1932. Learn all you can about the artists and their work. Make the calendar images live before the eyes of your prospect customers." (Authors' collection.)

Fletcher Ransom was one of the company's dedicated artists who moved to Joliet and produced dozens of calendar images for a long career. He was born in 1870 in Alamo, Michigan. He attended both the Art Institute of Chicago and the Academy of Fine Arts in New York. He shared living quarters at one time with the notable Cy Young. He is best known for his images of Abraham Lincoln, which appear in many of his calendar illustrations. He also did illustrations for Cream of Wheat, *Collier's* magazine, and *Woman's Home Companion* magazine. He passed away in 1943 after moving back to Michigan. (Authors' collection.)

This print, titled *On Top of the World*, was in the 1931 Gerlach Barklow calendar line. The artist was Chester K. Van Nortwick. The calendar company story that went with this print states, "That On Top of the World, Feeling! We've all had it. Christmas Eve, birthdays, paydays, when we make a hole in one . . . and Spring. For instance, the girl in this picture. It was Spring. May the picture, and calendar which it adores, mean for many days of unending happiness and joyous pleasure of feeling On Top of the World. C. K. Van Nortwick has given to us a bit of sunshine and Spring to help retain that feeling throughout the year." Van Nortwick did numerous images for Gerlach Barklow, including images for its Volland book line. The Volland books included images of Jack and the Beanstalk, Humpty Dumpty, and Mother Goose. (Authors' collection.)

Erma Chuk began collecting Gerlach Barklow Company prints long before it was popular with illustration art collectors. Early on, she recognized the beauty and quality of the artwork produced by these artists and the calendar factory. She thought of even the smallest print as one of her treasures. Much like the authors, she never grew tired of admiring the prints in her collection. Erma Chuk gave presentations to various audiences on the Gerlach Barklow Company, even after reaching over 90 years of age. She should be credited with being a major reason that the details of both the calendar company and the artists are well known today. She had a vision of one day assembling a Gerlach Barklow reference book with a few other collectors. It is hoped that this book does justice to her vision. (Authors' collection.)

Nicholas C. Georges was always enthusiastic about finding one of his Gerlach Barklow lady prints at a local auction, antique store, or even a Joliet-area garage sale. He truly loved the pretty woman calendar prints that were signed by his favorite artists, including Zula Kenyon, Adelaide Hiebel, Bradshaw Crandell, or Haskell Coffin. Nicholas C. Georges always talked Gerlach Barklow with the authors, teaching them to have fun while collecting. He loved visiting with the other attendees at the auctions or sales. A perfect gentleman to all he met, he was much loved by the local collecting community. Collectors across America would be astonished by the massive beautiful collection that this wonderful local farmer collected over the years. Joliet will miss this true gentleman who passionately collected Gerlach Barklow Company memorabilia. (Courtesy of the Nicholas C. Georges family.)

Bibliography

Driscoll, Barbara, Chuck Kahle, Norm Platnick, and Tim Smith. *Love's Old Sweet Song: A Collector's Guide to Zula Kenyon*. Bay Shore, NY: Enchantment Ink, 2004.

Huisking, Richard, Jr., and Norm Platnick. *The Winsome Lass: A Collector's Guide to Haskell Coffin*. Bay Shore, NY: Enchantment Ink, 2003.

Kahle, Chuck, Norm Platnick, and Tim Smith. *The Old, Old Story: A Collector's Guide to Adelaide Hiebel*. Bay Shore, NY: Enchantment Ink, 2004.

Martin, Charlotte, and Rick Martin. *Vintage Illustration: Discovering America's Calendar Artists, 1900–1960*. Portland, OR: Collectors Press, 1997.

Platnick, Norman I. *Roses of Romance: A Collector's Guide to Bradshaw Crandell*. Bay Shore, NY: Enchantment Ink, 2003.

Visit us at
arcadiapublishing.com

....

www.ingramcontent.com/pod-product-compliance
Lightning Source LLC
Chambersburg PA
CBHW050641110426
42813CB00007B/1881